Halloween Cupcake Recipe Ideas

Stir Up Some Magic with These Enchanting Cupcake Creations and Craft Unforgettable Moments

MATTHEW REYNOLDS

© Copyright 2023 by Matthew Reynolds – All rights reserved.

This book, including all of its content, is protected by copyright laws and international copyright treaties. Unauthorized use, reproduction, or distribution of any part of this book is prohibited.

Any person who engages in the unauthorized distribution, reproduction, or use of this book may be liable for civil and/or criminal penalties under applicable copyright laws.

For permission to use any part of this book, please contact the author or the publisher.

Disclaimer

The information provided in this book is for general informational purposes only. While every effort has been made to provide accurate and up-to-date information, the author and publisher make no representations or warranties of any kind, express or implied, about the completeness, accuracy, reliability, suitability, or availability of the information contained within this book. Any reliance you place on such information is strictly at your own risk.

Allergies: The recipes included in this book may contain a wide variety of ingredients, and some of them may be common allergens, such as nuts, soy, wheat, or others. It is crucial for readers to be aware of their own allergies and the allergies of those for whom they are preparing food. While efforts have been made to identify potential allergens in the recipes, the author and publisher cannot guarantee that allergenic ingredients are not present in trace amounts due to cross-contamination or other factors.

The author and publisher strongly recommend that readers with known food allergies exercise caution and consult with a qualified healthcare professional or allergist before preparing and consuming any recipe from this book. It is the responsibility of the reader to verify the ingredients used and to make informed decisions regarding their dietary choices.

The author and publisher shall not be held liable for any loss, damage, or injury resulting from the use or misuse of the information presented in this book, including allergic reactions. The author and publisher do not endorse any specific products, brands, or services mentioned in this book.

Medical Advice: The recipes and nutritional information provided in this book are intended for educational and illustrative purposes only. They are not meant to substitute for professional dietary, nutritional, or medical advice. Readers are encouraged to consult with a qualified healthcare or nutrition professional before making dietary or lifestyle changes, especially if they have specific dietary restrictions, allergies, or medical conditions

All rights reserved. No part of this book may be reproduced, distributed, or transmitted in any form or by any means, including photocopying, recording, or other electronic or mechanical methods, without the prior written permission of the author, except in the case of brief quotations embodied in critical reviews and certain other non-commercial uses permitted by copyright law.

Loved the book? Don't forget to leave a review.

Check out my Amazon profile for more Halloween recipe books.

Table of Contents

Witch's Brew Cupcakes 14

Monster Mash Cupcakes 16

Vampire Velvet Cupcakes 18

Ghostly White Chocolate Cupcakes 20

Mummy Mint Chocolate Cupcakes 22

Candy Corn Surprise Cupcakes 24

Spiderweb Peanut Butter Cupcakes 26

Haunted Pumpkin Spice Cupcakes 28

Zombie Brain Red Velvet Cupcakes 30

Caramel Apple Cupcakes 32

Skeleton Bone Vanilla Cupcakes 34

Midnight Blackberry Cupcakes 36

Frankenstein's Green Tea Cupcakes 38

Bat Wing Banana Cupcakes 40

Swampy Pistachio Cupcakes 42

Eyeball Lemon Cupcakes 44

Candy Corn Muffin Cupcakes 46

Cursed Carrot Cupcakes 48

Poison Apple Cinnamon Cupcakes 51

Oreo Spider Cupcakes 53

Candy Cauldron Cupcakes 55

Pumpkin Cheesecake Cupcakes 57

Jack-O'-Lantern Spice Cupcakes 60

Creepy Crawly Coconut Cupcakes 62

Werewolf Walnut Cupcakes 64

Slime-Filled Strawberry Cupcakes 66

Ghostly Marshmallow Cupcakes 68

Wicked Witch Matcha Cupcakes 70

Bloody Vampire Red Velvet Cupcakes 72

Swamp Monster Mint Chocolate Cupcakes 74

Mummy Wrapped Banana Cupcakes 76

Spooky Spiderweb Cheesecake Cupcakes 78

Candy-Coated Pretzel Cupcakes 80

Vampire Bite Red Velvet Cupcakes 82

Monster Eyeball Cupcakes..84

Haunted Graveyard Cupcakes 86

Witch's Brew Cupcakes 88

Pumpkin Patch Chocolate Cupcakes 90

Ghostly Peanut Butter Cup Cupcakes 92

Candy Corn Buttercream Cupcakes 94

Witches' Hat Chocolate Cupcakes..96

Pumpkin Spice Latte Cupcakes 98

Frankenstein's Monster Mint Cupcakes.....................................100

Spider's Nest Chocolate Cupcakes 102

Caramel Apple Cupcakes 104

Eyeball Pudding-Filled Cupcakes 106

Black Cat Chocolate Cupcakes 108

Jack-o'-Lantern Pumpkin Cupcakes 110

Zombie Brain Raspberry Cupcakes 112

Haunted Castle Cookie Cupcakes 114

Midnight Pumpkin Cupcakes 116

Witch's Cauldron Chocolate Cupcakes 118

Spiderweb White Chocolate Cupcakes 120

Candy Corn Vanilla Cupcakes 122

Bloody Vampire Bite Cupcakes 124

Ghostly Marshmallow Cupcakes 126

Mummy Wrapped Banana Cupcakes 128

Poison Apple Caramel Cupcakes 130

Bat Chocolate Cherry Cupcakes 132

Skeleton Bone Vanilla Cupcakes 134

Pumpkin Patch Cream Cheese Cupcakes 136

Slime-Filled Alien Cupcakes 138

Gory Brain Chocolate Cupcakes 140

Creepy Crawler Oreo Cupcakes 142

Wicked Witch Potion Cupcakes 144

Haunted House Chocolate Cupcakes 146

Pumpkin Spice Latte Cupcakes 148

Frankenstein's Monster Mint Cupcakes 150

Swamp Creature Green Tea Cupcakes 152

Candy Apple Cinnamon Cupcakes 154

Spooky Eyeball Red Velvet Cupcakes 156

Witch's Broomstick Chocolate Cupcakes 158

Caramel Apple Streusel Cupcakes 160

Melted Witch Chocolate Cupcakes 162

Pumpkin Pie Spice Cupcakes 164

Creepy Crawly Spiderweb Cupcakes 166

Monster Mash Banana Cupcakes 168

Candy Corn Creamsicle Cupcakes 170

Vampire Bite Red Velvet Cupcakes 172

Pumpkin Patch Chocolate Cupcakes 174

Spiderweb Chocolate Orange Cupcakes 176

Caramel Apple Crisp Cupcakes 178

Pumpkin Spice Latte Cupcakes 180

Frankenstein's Monster Mint Cupcakes 182

Swamp Creature Green Tea Cupcakes 184

Candy Apple Cinnamon Cupcakes 186

Witches' Brew Green Punch 188

Candy Corn Fruit Parfait 190

Ghostly Banana Pops 192

Pumpkin Pie Dip with Apple Slices 194

Ghostly Meringue Cookies 196

Caramel Apple Dip 198

Pumpkin Spice Popcorn 200

Spiderweb Guacamole 202

Mummy Hot Dogs 204

Haunted Halloween Punch 206

Witch Hat Cookies 208

Pumpkin Rice Krispie Treats 210

Creepy Crawly Deviled Eggs 212

Candy Corn Jello Cups 214

Thank you 216

Witch's Brew Cupcakes

Ingredients:

- 1 box of chocolate cake mix
- 3 eggs
- 1/2 cup vegetable oil
- 1 cup water
- Green food coloring
- Witch hat decorations (optional)

Instructions:

1. Preheat your oven to 350°F (175°C) and line a cupcake pan with liners.
2. In a mixing bowl, combine the cake mix, eggs, vegetable oil, and water. Mix until smooth.
3. Add green food coloring until you achieve a witchy brew color.
4. Pour the batter into the cupcake liners, filling each about 2/3 full.

5. Bake for 18-20 minutes or until a toothpick inserted comes out clean.

6. Let the cupcakes cool in the pan for 5 minutes, then transfer them to a wire rack to cool completely.

7. Once cooled, decorate with witch hat decorations if desired.

Summary: Witch's Brew Cupcakes are chocolatey treats with a spooky twist, perfect for Halloween. They're easy to make and can be customized with witch hat decorations for added flair.

Tips and Tricks:

- Adjust the amount of green food coloring to achieve your desired "brew" color.

- You can make your own witch hat decorations using black fondant or purchase them from a baking supply store.

Monster Mash Cupcakes

Ingredients:

- 1 box of vanilla cake mix
- 3 eggs
- 1/2 cup butter, softened
- 1 cup milk
- Green, purple, and orange food coloring
- Candy eyeballs
- Gummy worms

Instructions:

1. Preheat your oven to 350°F (175°C) and line a cupcake pan with liners.
2. In a mixing bowl, combine the cake mix, eggs, softened butter, and milk. Mix until well combined.
3. Divide the batter into three portions and dye one portion green, one purple, and one orange.
4. Fill each cupcake liner with a spoonful of each colored batter, creating a marbled effect.

5. Bake for 18-20 minutes or until a toothpick inserted comes out clean.

6. Let the cupcakes cool, then decorate with candy eyeballs and gummy worms.

Summary: Monster Mash Cupcakes are a colorful and fun Halloween treat with a surprise inside. The marbled cake batter and spooky decorations make them a hit at parties.

Tips and Tricks:

- Use gel food coloring for vibrant colors.
- Experiment with different candy decorations like mini chocolate chips or licorice.

Vampire Velvet Cupcakes

Ingredients:

- 1 box of red velvet cake mix
- 3 eggs
- 1/2 cup vegetable oil
- 1 cup buttermilk
- Cream cheese frosting
- Edible vampire fangs

Instructions:

1. Preheat your oven to 350ºF (175ºC) and line a cupcake pan with liners.
2. In a mixing bowl, combine the red velvet cake mix, eggs, vegetable oil, and buttermilk. Mix until smooth.
3. Fill each cupcake liner 2/3 full with the batter.
4. Bake for 18-20 minutes or until a toothpick inserted comes out clean.
5. Let the cupcakes cool completely.

6. Frost the cupcakes with cream cheese frosting.

7. Insert edible vampire fangs into the frosting for a spooky touch.

Summary: Vampire Velvet Cupcakes are blood-red delights perfect for a Halloween party. The red velvet cake pairs wonderfully with cream cheese frosting and edible vampire fangs.

Tips and Tricks:

- Make your own edible vampire fangs using almond slices and red gel food coloring.
- Use a piping bag for a neater frosting application.

Ghostly White Chocolate Cupcakes

Ingredients:

- 1 box of white cake mix
- 3 eggs
- 1/2 cup unsalted butter, melted
- 1 cup milk
- White chocolate chips
- White chocolate ganache
- Edible googly eyes

Instructions:

1. Preheat your oven to 350°F (175°C) and line a cupcake pan with liners.
2. In a mixing bowl, combine the white cake mix, eggs, melted butter, and milk. Mix until well combined.
3. Fold in white chocolate chips to the batter.
4. Fill each cupcake liner 2/3 full with the batter.

5. Bake for 18-20 minutes or until a toothpick inserted comes out clean.

6. Let the cupcakes cool completely.

7. Drizzle white chocolate ganache over each cupcake and add edible googly eyes for a ghostly effect.

Summary: Ghostly White Chocolate Cupcakes are spooky and sweet, featuring white chocolate chips, ganache, and edible googly eyes. Perfect for Halloween!

Tips and Tricks:

- You can use store-bought edible googly eyes or make your own with white chocolate and mini chocolate chips.

- Use caution when melting white chocolate to avoid burning it.

Mummy Mint Chocolate Cupcakes

Ingredients:

- 1 box of chocolate mint cake mix
- 3 eggs
- 1/2 cup vegetable oil
- 1 cup water
- White frosting
- Candy eyeballs

Instructions:

1. Preheat your oven to 350°F (175°C) and line a cupcake pan with liners.
2. In a mixing bowl, combine the chocolate mint cake mix, eggs, vegetable oil, and water. Mix until smooth.
3. Fill each cupcake liner 2/3 full with the batter.
4. Bake for 18-20 minutes or until a toothpick inserted comes out clean.
5. Let the cupcakes cool completely.

6. Frost each cupcake with white frosting.

7. Place candy eyeballs on top to create the mummy's eyes.

Summary: Mummy Mint Chocolate Cupcakes are a delightful combination of chocolate and mint with a spooky mummy twist. The candy eyeballs add a fun touch.

Tips and Tricks:

- Experiment with different flavors of cake mix for unique variations.
- Use a piping bag with a flat tip for easy frosting.

Candy Corn Surprise Cupcakes

Ingredients:

- 1 box of yellow cake mix
- 3 eggs
- 1/2 cup vegetable oil
- 1 cup water
- Candy corn
- Orange and yellow frosting

Instructions:

1. Preheat your oven to 350°F (175°C) and line a cupcake pan with liners.
2. In a mixing bowl, combine the yellow cake mix, eggs, vegetable oil, and water. Mix until well combined.
3. Fill each cupcake liner 1/3 full with batter.
4. Drop a candy corn into each cupcake.
5. Cover the candy corn with more batter, filling each liner about 2/3 full.

6. Bake for 18-20 minutes or until a toothpick inserted comes out clean.

7. Let the cupcakes cool completely.

8. Frost the cupcakes with orange and yellow frosting in a candy corn pattern.

Summary: Candy Corn Surprise Cupcakes hide a sweet surprise inside. They're colorful, festive, and perfect for Halloween celebrations.

Tips and Tricks:

- You can also add a small amount of candy corn to the frosting for extra flavor and decoration.

- Make sure to completely cool the cupcakes before frosting to prevent melting.

Spiderweb Peanut Butter Cupcakes

Ingredients:

- 1 box of peanut butter cake mix
- 3 eggs
- 1/2 cup vegetable oil
- 1 cup milk
- Peanut butter frosting
- Black icing gel

Instructions:

1. Preheat your oven to 350°F (175°C) and line a cupcake pan with liners.
2. In a mixing bowl, combine the peanut butter cake mix, eggs, vegetable oil, and milk. Mix until smooth.
3. Fill each cupcake liner 2/3 full with the batter.
4. Bake for 18-20 minutes or until a toothpick inserted comes out clean.
5. Let the cupcakes cool completely.
6. Frost each cupcake with peanut butter frosting.

7. Use black icing gel to draw spiderwebs on top of the frosting.

Summary: Spiderweb Peanut Butter Cupcakes are a delicious combination of peanut butter flavor and spooky spiderweb decorations. Perfect for Halloween parties!

Tips and Tricks:

- You can use a toothpick to help create intricate spiderweb designs with the black icing gel.
- If you're short on time, use store-bought peanut butter frosting.

Haunted Pumpkin Spice Cupcakes

Ingredients:

- 1 box of pumpkin spice cake mix
- 3 eggs
- 1/2 cup vegetable oil
- 1 cup canned pumpkin puree
- Cream cheese frosting
- Pumpkin-shaped sprinkles

Instructions:

1. Preheat your oven to 350°F (175°C) and line a cupcake pan with liners.
2. In a mixing bowl, combine the pumpkin spice cake mix, eggs, vegetable oil, and canned pumpkin puree. Mix until well combined.
3. Fill each cupcake liner 2/3 full with the batter.
4. Bake for 18-20 minutes or until a toothpick inserted comes out clean.
5. Let the cupcakes cool completely.

6. Frost each cupcake with cream cheese frosting.

7. Decorate with pumpkin-shaped sprinkles for a festive touch.

Summary: Haunted Pumpkin Spice Cupcakes capture the flavors of fall with pumpkin spice and cream cheese frosting. They're a perfect treat for Halloween gatherings.

Tips and Tricks:

- You can add a pinch of cinnamon and nutmeg to enhance the pumpkin spice flavor.

- If you prefer a homemade cream cheese frosting, feel free to make one from scratch.

Zombie Brain Red Velvet Cupcakes

Ingredients:

- 1 box of red velvet cake mix
- 3 eggs
- 1/2 cup vegetable oil
- 1 cup buttermilk
- Red raspberry jam
- Edible "brain" decorations (made from red fondant)

Instructions:

1. Preheat your oven to 350°F (175°C) and line a cupcake pan with liners.
2. In a mixing bowl, combine the red velvet cake mix, eggs, vegetable oil, and buttermilk. Mix until smooth.
3. Fill each cupcake liner 2/3 full with the batter.
4. Bake for 18-20 minutes or until a toothpick inserted comes out clean.

5. Let the cupcakes cool completely.

6. Use a small spoon to create a hollow in the center of each cupcake.

7. Fill the hollow with red raspberry jam to resemble "zombie brains."

8. Decorate with edible fondant brain decorations.

Summary: Zombie Brain Red Velvet Cupcakes are a gruesome yet delicious Halloween treat. The red velvet cake and raspberry jam filling create a creepy effect.

Tips and Tricks:

- Make the fondant brain decorations in advance and let them dry before placing them on the cupcakes.

- You can also use strawberry or cherry jam for a different "brain" look.

Caramel Apple Cupcakes

Ingredients:

- 1 box of apple spice cake mix
- 3 eggs
- 1/2 cup unsalted butter, melted
- 1 cup apple sauce
- Caramel sauce
- Chopped peanuts (optional)

Instructions:

1. Preheat your oven to 350°F (175°C) and line a cupcake pan with liners.
2. In a mixing bowl, combine the apple spice cake mix, eggs, melted butter, and apple sauce. Mix until well combined.
3. Fill each cupcake liner 2/3 full with the batter.
4. Bake for 18-20 minutes or until a toothpick inserted comes out clean.
5. Let the cupcakes cool completely.

6. Drizzle caramel sauce over each cupcake and sprinkle with chopped peanuts if desired.

Summary: Caramel Apple Cupcakes capture the essence of fall with apple spice cake, caramel sauce, and optional peanuts. They're a delicious Halloween treat.

Tips and Tricks:

- You can also use store-bought caramel sauce, or make your own by melting caramel candies with a splash of milk.

- If allergies are a concern, omit the nuts or use a nut-free topping.

Skeleton Bone Vanilla Cupcakes

Ingredients:

- 1 box of vanilla cake mix
- 3 eggs
- 1/2 cup vegetable oil
- 1 cup milk
- White frosting
- Pretzel sticks (for "bones")

Instructions:

1. Preheat your oven to 350°F (175°C) and line a cupcake pan with liners.
2. In a mixing bowl, combine the vanilla cake mix, eggs, vegetable oil, and milk. Mix until well combined.
3. Fill each cupcake liner 2/3 full with the batter.
4. Bake for 18-20 minutes or until a toothpick inserted comes out clean.
5. Let the cupcakes cool completely.

6. Frost each cupcake with white frosting.

7. Break pretzel sticks into smaller pieces and insert them into the cupcakes to resemble skeleton bones.

Summary: Skeleton Bone Vanilla Cupcakes are a fun and spooky Halloween treat. Pretzel sticks turn them into edible skeletons!

Tips and Tricks:

- Be gentle when inserting the pretzel sticks to avoid breaking the cupcakes.
- Use a piping bag for precise frosting application.

Midnight Blackberry Cupcakes

Ingredients:

- 1 box of blackberry cake mix
- 3 eggs
- 1/2 cup vegetable oil
- 1 cup buttermilk
- Blackberry jam
- Purple frosting
- Fresh blackberries (for garnish)

Instructions:

1. Preheat your oven to 350°F (175°C) and line a cupcake pan with liners.
2. In a mixing bowl, combine the blackberry cake mix, eggs, vegetable oil, and buttermilk. Mix until smooth.
3. Fill each cupcake liner 2/3 full with the batter.
4. Bake for 18-20 minutes or until a toothpick inserted comes out clean.

5. Let the cupcakes cool completely.

6. Use a small spoon to create a hollow in the center of each cupcake.

7. Fill the hollow with blackberry jam.

8. Frost the cupcakes with purple frosting and garnish with fresh blackberries.

Summary: Midnight Blackberry Cupcakes are a fruity and elegant Halloween treat. The combination of blackberry cake, jam filling, and fresh blackberries is simply delightful.

Tips and Tricks:

- You can use blackberry preserves instead of jam for a smoother filling.

- If fresh blackberries are not available, you can use frozen ones or omit them.

Frankenstein's Green Tea Cupcakes

Ingredients:

- 1 box of green tea matcha cake mix
- 3 eggs
- 1/2 cup vegetable oil
- 1 cup milk
- Green tea frosting
- Chocolate chips (for "bolts")

Instructions:

1. Preheat your oven to 350°F (175°C) and line a cupcake pan with liners.
2. In a mixing bowl, combine the green tea matcha cake mix, eggs, vegetable oil, and milk. Mix until well combined.
3. Fill each cupcake liner 2/3 full with the batter.
4. Bake for 18-20 minutes or until a toothpick inserted comes out clean.
5. Let the cupcakes cool completely.

6. Frost each cupcake with green tea frosting.

7. Insert chocolate chips into the sides of the cupcakes to resemble Frankenstein's bolts.

Summary: Frankenstein's Green Tea Cupcakes are a unique and flavorful Halloween treat. The green tea matcha flavor pairs perfectly with the spooky Frankenstein theme.

Tips and Tricks:

- Use dark chocolate chips for a more pronounced "bolt" effect.

- You can make your own green tea frosting by mixing matcha powder into vanilla frosting.

Bat Wing Banana Cupcakes

Ingredients:

- 1 box of banana cake mix
- 3 eggs
- 1/2 cup vegetable oil
- 1 cup mashed ripe bananas
- Chocolate bat wing decorations (made from melted chocolate)

Instructions:

1. Preheat your oven to 350°F (175°C) and line a cupcake pan with liners.
2. In a mixing bowl, combine the banana cake mix, eggs, vegetable oil, and mashed bananas. Mix until well combined.
3. Fill each cupcake liner 2/3 full with the batter.
4. Bake for 18-20 minutes or until a toothpick inserted comes out clean.
5. Let the cupcakes cool completely.

6. Prepare chocolate bat wing decorations by melting chocolate and shaping it into bat wing shapes. Allow them to harden.

7. Once the cupcakes are cool, gently insert the chocolate bat wings into the tops.

Summary: Bat Wing Banana Cupcakes are a whimsical and tasty Halloween treat with a banana twist. The chocolate bat wings add a fun and spooky element.

Tips and Tricks:

- Use ripe bananas for the best banana flavor in the cupcakes.

- Make the chocolate bat wings in advance to ensure they are fully set before inserting them.

Swampy Pistachio Cupcakes

Ingredients:

- 1 box of pistachio cake mix
- 3 eggs
- 1/2 cup vegetable oil
- 1 cup milk
- Green pistachio pudding frosting
- Crushed pistachios (for garnish)

Instructions:

1. Preheat your oven to 350°F (175°C) and line a cupcake pan with liners.
2. In a mixing bowl, combine the pistachio cake mix, eggs, vegetable oil, and milk. Mix until well combined.
3. Fill each cupcake liner 2/3 full with the batter.
4. Bake for 18-20 minutes or until a toothpick inserted comes out clean.
5. Let the cupcakes cool completely.

6. Frost the cupcakes with green pistachio pudding frosting.

7. Garnish with crushed pistachios for a swampy texture.

Summary: Swampy Pistachio Cupcakes are a nutty and unique Halloween treat. The pistachio cake and pudding frosting create a deliciously green and swampy look.

Tips and Tricks:

- You can enhance the green color of the frosting with a drop or two of green food coloring.

- Toast the crushed pistachios for a richer flavor and crunchier texture.

Eyeball Lemon Cupcakes

Ingredients:

- 1 box of lemon cake mix
- 3 eggs
- 1/2 cup vegetable oil
- 1 cup buttermilk
- Lemon frosting
- Candy eyeballs

Instructions:

1. Preheat your oven to 350°F (175°C) and line a cupcake pan with liners.
2. In a mixing bowl, combine the lemon cake mix, eggs, vegetable oil, and buttermilk. Mix until smooth.
3. Fill each cupcake liner 2/3 full with the batter.
4. Bake for 18-20 minutes or until a toothpick inserted comes out clean.
5. Let the cupcakes cool completely.

6. Frost each cupcake with lemon frosting.

7. Place candy eyeballs on top to create eerie "eyeballs."

Summary: Eyeball Lemon Cupcakes are a zesty and fun Halloween treat. The lemony flavor pairs perfectly with the candy eyeball decorations.

Tips and Tricks:

- You can add lemon zest to the frosting for extra lemon flavor.

- Make sure the cupcakes are fully cooled before frosting to prevent melting.

Candy Corn Muffin Cupcakes

Ingredients:

- 1 box of cornbread muffin mix
- 1/2 cup milk
- 1/4 cup melted butter
- 1/4 cup honey
- Yellow and orange food coloring
- Candy corn (for garnish)

Instructions:

1. Preheat your oven to 375°F (190°C) and line a cupcake pan with liners.
2. In a mixing bowl, prepare the cornbread muffin mix according to package instructions, using milk, melted butter, and honey.
3. Divide the batter into three portions. Leave one portion plain, dye one portion yellow, and dye the other portion orange.
4. Layer the three colors in each cupcake liner, starting with plain, then yellow, and finally orange.

5. Bake for 15-18 minutes or until the tops are golden brown.

6. Let the muffin cupcakes cool.

7. Garnish each cupcake with candy corn.

Summary: Candy Corn Muffin Cupcakes put a sweet twist on classic cornbread muffins. They are a colorful and festive treat for Halloween.

Tips and Tricks:

- Use gel food coloring for vibrant colors.
- Adjust the amount of honey to your preferred level of sweetness.

Cursed Carrot Cupcakes

Ingredients:

- 1 cup grated carrots
- 1/2 cup crushed pineapple, drained
- 1/2 cup raisins
- 1/2 cup chopped walnuts
- 1 1/2 cups all-purpose flour
- 1 tsp baking powder
- 1/2 tsp baking soda
- 1/2 tsp salt
- 1 tsp ground cinnamon
- 1/2 tsp ground nutmeg
- 1/4 cup vegetable oil
- 1/2 cup granulated sugar
- 1/2 cup brown sugar
- 2 eggs
- Cream cheese frosting

Instructions:

1. Preheat your oven to 350°F (175°C) and line a cupcake pan with liners.
2. In a bowl, combine grated carrots, crushed pineapple, raisins, and chopped walnuts. Set aside.
3. In another bowl, whisk together flour, baking powder, baking soda, salt, cinnamon, and nutmeg.
4. In a separate large bowl, beat together vegetable oil, granulated sugar, brown sugar, and eggs until well combined.
5. Gradually add the dry ingredients to the wet ingredients, mixing until smooth.
6. Fold in the carrot mixture until evenly distributed.
7. Fill each cupcake liner 2/3 full with the batter.
8. Bake for 18-20 minutes or until a toothpick inserted comes out clean.
9. Let the cupcakes cool completely.
10. Frost with cream cheese frosting.

Summary: Cursed Carrot Cupcakes are a wholesome and spiced treat perfect for Halloween. The combination of carrots, pineapple, raisins, and nuts creates a deliciously cursed flavor.

Tips and Tricks:

- If you prefer, you can use a different frosting such as vanilla or cinnamon cream cheese frosting.
- Add a dash of ginger for an extra layer of spice.

Poison Apple Cinnamon Cupcakes

Ingredients:

- 1 box of cinnamon cake mix
- 3 eggs
- 1/2 cup vegetable oil
- 1 cup water
- Red apple-shaped gummies (for garnish)
- Caramel sauce

Instructions:

1. Preheat your oven to 350°F (175°C) and line a cupcake pan with liners.
2. In a mixing bowl, combine the cinnamon cake mix, eggs, vegetable oil, and water. Mix until smooth.
3. Fill each cupcake liner 2/3 full with the batter.
4. Bake for 18-20 minutes or until a toothpick inserted comes out clean.
5. Let the cupcakes cool completely.
6. Drizzle caramel sauce over each cupcake.

7. Garnish with red apple-shaped gummies.

Summary: Poison Apple Cinnamon Cupcakes are a delectable blend of cinnamon cake and caramel sauce, with a wickedly fun apple garnish.

Tips and Tricks:

- If you can't find apple-shaped gummies, you can use apple-shaped cookie decorations or fondant cutouts.

- Warm the caramel sauce slightly for easier drizzling.

Oreo Spider Cupcakes

Ingredients:

- 1 box of chocolate cake mix
- 3 eggs
- 1/2 cup vegetable oil
- 1 cup water
- Chocolate frosting
- Chocolate sandwich cookies (e.g., Oreos)
- Black licorice (for spider legs)

Instructions:

1. Preheat your oven to 350°F (175°C) and line a cupcake pan with liners.
2. In a mixing bowl, combine the chocolate cake mix, eggs, vegetable oil, and water. Mix until smooth.
3. Fill each cupcake liner 2/3 full with the batter.
4. Bake for 18-20 minutes or until a toothpick inserted comes out clean.
5. Let the cupcakes cool completely.

6. Frost each cupcake with chocolate frosting.

7. Separate the chocolate sandwich cookies, removing the cream centers.

8. Insert four pieces of black licorice into each side of the cream center to create spider legs.

9. Place the spider "body" (cream center) on top of each cupcake.

Summary: Oreo Spider Cupcakes are a creepy-crawly Halloween treat with a delicious chocolatey flavor. The Oreo spiders add a spooky touch.

Tips and Tricks:

- Use edible googly eyes for an extra fun and creepy effect.

- Be gentle when inserting the licorice legs to prevent them from breaking.

Candy Cauldron Cupcakes

Ingredients:

- 1 box of chocolate cake mix
- 3 eggs
- 1/2 cup vegetable oil
- 1 cup water
- Chocolate frosting
- Black licorice (for cauldron handles)
- Assorted Halloween candies (for cauldron filling)

Instructions:

1. Preheat your oven to 350°F (175°C) and line a cupcake pan with liners.
2. In a mixing bowl, combine the chocolate cake mix, eggs, vegetable oil, and water. Mix until smooth.
3. Fill each cupcake liner 2/3 full with the batter.
4. Bake for 18-20 minutes or until a toothpick inserted comes out clean.
5. Let the cupcakes cool completely.

6. Frost each cupcake with chocolate frosting.

7. Insert small pieces of black licorice into each side of the cupcake to create cauldron handles.

8. Fill each cupcake with assorted Halloween candies to resemble a candy cauldron.

Summary: Candy Cauldron Cupcakes are a sweet and creative Halloween treat. The candy-filled cauldrons are a delightful surprise.

Tips and Tricks:

- Choose a variety of colorful Halloween candies for the cauldron filling.

- You can use melted chocolate or frosting to secure the licorice handles if needed.

Pumpkin Cheesecake Cupcakes

Ingredients:

- 1 cup graham cracker crumbs
- 2 tbsp melted butter
- 1 1/2 cups cream cheese
- 1/2 cup granulated sugar
- 1 tsp vanilla extract
- 2 eggs
- 1 cup canned pumpkin puree
- 1/2 tsp pumpkin pie spice
- Whipped cream (for topping)
- Ground cinnamon (for garnish)

Instructions:

1. Preheat your oven to 325°F (160°C) and line a cupcake pan with liners.
2. In a bowl, combine graham cracker crumbs and melted butter. Press a spoonful of the mixture into

the bottom of each cupcake liner to create the crust.

3. In a separate bowl, beat together cream cheese, granulated sugar, and vanilla extract until smooth.

4. Add eggs one at a time, mixing well after each addition.

5. Pour half of the cream cheese mixture over the crust in each cupcake liner.

6. In another bowl, mix together canned pumpkin puree and pumpkin pie spice.

7. Carefully spoon the pumpkin mixture on top of the cream cheese layer in each liner.

8. Bake for 20-25 minutes or until the centers are set.

9. Let the cupcakes cool, then refrigerate for at least 2 hours.

10. Top with whipped cream and a sprinkle of ground cinnamon before serving.

Summary: Pumpkin Cheesecake Cupcakes are a delightful blend of creamy cheesecake and pumpkin spice flavors, perfect for a Halloween dessert.

Tips and Tricks:

- You can use pre-made graham cracker crusts for convenience.

- For a richer flavor, use freshly roasted pumpkin puree instead of canned.

Jack-O'-Lantern Spice Cupcakes

Ingredients:

- 1 box of spiced cake mix
- 3 eggs
- 1/2 cup vegetable oil
- 1 cup water
- Orange frosting
- Black decorating gel
- Candy corn (for garnish)

Instructions:

1. Preheat your oven to 350°F (175°C) and line a cupcake pan with liners.
2. In a mixing bowl, combine the spiced cake mix, eggs, vegetable oil, and water. Mix until smooth.
3. Fill each cupcake liner 2/3 full with the batter.
4. Bake for 18-20 minutes or until a toothpick inserted comes out clean.
5. Let the cupcakes cool completely.

6. Frost each cupcake with orange frosting.

7. Use black decorating gel to draw jack-o'-lantern faces on top of the frosting.

8. Garnish with candy corn for added Halloween flair.

Summary: Jack-O'-Lantern Spice Cupcakes are a festive and spicy Halloween treat. The jack-o'-lantern faces add a playful touch.

Tips and Tricks:

- To make drawing the faces easier, you can use toothpicks or small paintbrushes with the black decorating gel.

- Get creative with your jack-o'-lantern expressions!

Creepy Crawly Coconut Cupcakes

Ingredients:

- 1 box of coconut cake mix
- 3 eggs
- 1/2 cup vegetable oil
- 1 cup coconut milk
- Coconut frosting
- Gummy insects (e.g., worms, spiders)

Instructions:

1. Preheat your oven to 350°F (175°C) and line a cupcake pan with liners.
2. In a mixing bowl, combine the coconut cake mix, eggs, vegetable oil, and coconut milk. Mix until smooth.
3. Fill each cupcake liner 2/3 full with the batter.
4. Bake for 18-20 minutes or until a toothpick inserted comes out clean.
5. Let the cupcakes cool completely.

6. Frost each cupcake with coconut frosting.

7. Decorate with gummy insects to create a creepy-crawly look.

Summary: Creepy Crawly Coconut Cupcakes are a tropical twist on Halloween treats. The coconut flavor and gummy insects make them delightfully spooky.

Tips and Tricks:

- You can tint the coconut frosting with green food coloring for a swampy appearance.

- Place gummy insects strategically to create a lifelike effect.

Werewolf Walnut Cupcakes

Ingredients:

- 1 box of walnut cake mix
- 3 eggs
- 1/2 cup vegetable oil
- 1 cup milk
- Walnut frosting
- Chopped walnuts (for garnish)
- Edible werewolf teeth decorations

Instructions:

1. Preheat your oven to 350°F (175°C) and line a cupcake pan with liners.
2. In a mixing bowl, combine the walnut cake mix, eggs, vegetable oil, and milk. Mix until well combined.
3. Fill each cupcake liner 2/3 full with the batter.
4. Bake for 18-20 minutes or until a toothpick inserted comes out clean.

5. Let the cupcakes cool completely.

6. Frost each cupcake with walnut frosting.

7. Sprinkle chopped walnuts on top for added texture.

8. Place edible werewolf teeth decorations on the frosting.

Summary: Werewolf Walnut Cupcakes are a nutty and fun Halloween treat with a spooky twist. The edible werewolf teeth add a playful touch.

Tips and Tricks:

- You can make your own edible werewolf teeth decorations using white fondant or purchase them from a baking supply store.

- Toast the chopped walnuts for a richer flavor and crunchier texture.

Slime-Filled Strawberry Cupcakes

Ingredients:

- 1 box of strawberry cake mix
- 3 eggs
- 1/2 cup vegetable oil
- 1 cup water
- Strawberry frosting
- Green gel food coloring
- Edible slime (green fruit-flavored gel)

Instructions:

1. Preheat your oven to 350°F (175°C) and line a cupcake pan with liners.
2. In a mixing bowl, combine the strawberry cake mix, eggs, vegetable oil, and water. Mix until smooth.
3. Fill each cupcake liner 2/3 full with the batter.
4. Bake for 18-20 minutes or until a toothpick inserted comes out clean.
5. Let the cupcakes cool completely.

6. Frost each cupcake with strawberry frosting.

7. Tint the edible slime with green gel food coloring and place a small amount on top of each cupcake, allowing it to ooze down the sides.

Summary: Slime-Filled Strawberry Cupcakes are a playful and spooky Halloween treat. The strawberry and slime combination is both delicious and eerie.

Tips and Tricks:

- You can make the edible slime by mixing green fruit-flavored gel with a touch of corn syrup.

- Handle the edible slime with care to achieve the desired oozy effect.

Ghostly Marshmallow Cupcakes

Ingredients:

- 1 box of vanilla cake mix
- 3 eggs
- 1/2 cup vegetable oil
- 1 cup buttermilk
- Vanilla frosting
- Large marshmallows
- Black decorating gel

Instructions:

1. Preheat your oven to 350°F (175°C) and line a cupcake pan with liners.
2. In a mixing bowl, combine the vanilla cake mix, eggs, vegetable oil, and buttermilk. Mix until smooth.
3. Fill each cupcake liner 2/3 full with the batter.
4. Bake for 18-20 minutes or until a toothpick inserted comes out clean.

5. Let the cupcakes cool completely.

6. Frost each cupcake with vanilla frosting.

7. Place a large marshmallow on top of each cupcake.

8. Use black decorating gel to draw ghostly faces on the marshmallows.

Summary: Ghostly Marshmallow Cupcakes are a cute and spooky Halloween treat. The marshmallow ghosts add a fun and ghostly element.

Tips and Tricks:

- You can use edible googly eyes for the ghost faces.

- Warm the marshmallows slightly before drawing on them for better gel adherence.

Wicked Witch Matcha Cupcakes

Ingredients:

- 1 box of matcha green tea cake mix
- 3 eggs
- 1/2 cup vegetable oil
- 1 cup water
- Green tea frosting
- Witch hat cupcake toppers

Instructions:

1. Preheat your oven to 350°F (175°C) and line a cupcake pan with liners.
2. In a mixing bowl, combine the matcha green tea cake mix, eggs, vegetable oil, and water. Mix until well combined.
3. Fill each cupcake liner 2/3 full with the batter.
4. Bake for 18-20 minutes or until a toothpick inserted comes out clean.
5. Let the cupcakes cool completely.

6. Frost each cupcake with green tea frosting.

7. Place witch hat cupcake toppers on top for a wickedly delightful touch.

Summary: Wicked Witch Matcha Cupcakes are a unique and flavorful Halloween treat. The matcha green tea flavor adds an enchanting twist.

Tips and Tricks:

- You can make your own witch hat toppers from black fondant or purchase them from a baking supply store.

- Add a sprinkle of edible glitter for extra magic.

Bloody Vampire Red Velvet Cupcakes

Ingredients:

- 1 box of red velvet cake mix
- 3 eggs
- 1/2 cup vegetable oil
- 1 cup buttermilk
- Red fruit preserves or raspberry jam
- White frosting
- Edible vampire fang decorations

Instructions:

1. Preheat your oven to 350°F (175°C) and line a cupcake pan with liners.
2. In a mixing bowl, combine the red velvet cake mix, eggs, vegetable oil, and buttermilk. Mix until smooth.
3. Fill each cupcake liner 2/3 full with the batter.
4. Bake for 18-20 minutes or until a toothpick inserted comes out clean.

5. Let the cupcakes cool completely.

6. Use a small spoon to create a hollow in the center of each cupcake.

7. Fill the hollow with red fruit preserves or raspberry jam to resemble "bloody" filling.

8. Frost the cupcakes with white frosting.

9. Place edible vampire fang decorations on top.

Summary: Bloody Vampire Red Velvet Cupcakes are a spooky and delicious Halloween treat. The "bloody" filling and vampire fangs create a ghoulish effect.

Tips and Tricks:

- Make the hollows in the cupcakes large enough to hold a generous amount of "blood" filling.

- You can use cream cheese frosting for a different flavor profile.

Swamp Monster Mint Chocolate Cupcakes

Ingredients:

- 1 box of mint chocolate chip cake mix
- 3 eggs
- 1/2 cup vegetable oil
- 1 cup milk
- Mint chocolate frosting
- Green food coloring
- Gummy swamp creatures (e.g., alligators, frogs)

Instructions:

1. Preheat your oven to 350ºF (175ºC) and line a cupcake pan with liners.
2. In a mixing bowl, combine the mint chocolate chip cake mix, eggs, vegetable oil, and milk. Mix until well combined.
3. Add a few drops of green food coloring to tint the batter green and mix until evenly colored.

4. Fill each cupcake liner 2/3 full with the batter.
5. Bake for 18-20 minutes or until a toothpick inserted comes out clean.
6. Let the cupcakes cool completely.
7. Frost each cupcake with mint chocolate frosting.
8. Decorate with gummy swamp creatures for a spooky swamp monster theme.

Summary: Swamp Monster Mint Chocolate Cupcakes are a minty and spooky Halloween treat. The green tint and gummy swamp creatures make them perfect for a swampy theme.

Tips and Tricks:

- You can crush mint chocolate candies and sprinkle them on top for added texture.
- Refrigerate the cupcakes if the frosting becomes too soft due to warm weather.

Mummy Wrapped Banana Cupcakes

Ingredients:

- 1 box of banana cake mix
- 3 eggs
- 1/2 cup vegetable oil
- 1 cup mashed ripe bananas
- Cream cheese frosting
- Edible candy eyes
- White fondant (for mummy wraps)

Instructions:

1. Preheat your oven to 350°F (175°C) and line a cupcake pan with liners.

2. In a mixing bowl, combine the banana cake mix, eggs, vegetable oil, and mashed bananas. Mix until well combined.

3. Fill each cupcake liner 2/3 full with the batter.

4. Bake for 18-20 minutes or until a toothpick inserted comes out clean.

5. Let the cupcakes cool completely.

6. Frost each cupcake with cream cheese frosting.

7. Roll out small strips of white fondant and drape them over each cupcake to resemble mummy wraps.

8. Place edible candy eyes on top of the fondant strips.

Summary: Mummy Wrapped Banana Cupcakes are a playful and tasty Halloween treat. The mummy wraps and candy eyes create an adorable mummy theme.

Tips and Tricks:

- Make sure the fondant strips are thin enough to be easily eaten.

- If you don't have candy eyes, you can use small white candies or piped frosting dots.

Spooky Spiderweb Cheesecake Cupcakes

Ingredients:

- 1 cup graham cracker crumbs
- 2 tbsp melted butter
- 1 1/2 cups cream cheese
- 1/2 cup granulated sugar
- 1 tsp vanilla extract
- 2 eggs
- Chocolate icing gel (for spiderweb design)

Instructions:

1. Preheat your oven to 325°F (160°C) and line a cupcake pan with liners.
2. In a bowl, combine graham cracker crumbs and melted butter. Press a spoonful of the mixture into the bottom of each cupcake liner to create the crust.

3. In a separate bowl, beat together cream cheese, granulated sugar, and vanilla extract until smooth.

4. Add eggs one at a time, mixing well after each addition.

5. Pour the cream cheese mixture over the crust in each cupcake liner.

6. Bake for 20-25 minutes or until the centers are set.

7. Let the cheesecake cupcakes cool completely.

8. Use chocolate icing gel to create spiderweb designs on top of each cupcake.

Summary: Spooky Spiderweb Cheesecake Cupcakes are a decadent and festive Halloween dessert. The spiderweb design adds a spooky touch to creamy cheesecake.

Tips and Tricks:

- You can add a drop of black food coloring to the cheesecake batter for a darker color.

- Practice the spiderweb design on a piece of parchment paper before applying it to the cupcakes.

Candy-Coated Pretzel Cupcakes

Ingredients:

- 1 box of chocolate cake mix
- 3 eggs
- 1/2 cup vegetable oil
- 1 cup water
- Chocolate frosting
- Pretzel sticks
- Assorted Halloween candies (e.g., M&M's, Reese's Pieces)

Instructions:

1. Preheat your oven to 350°F (175°C) and line a cupcake pan with liners.
2. In a mixing bowl, combine the chocolate cake mix, eggs, vegetable oil, and water. Mix until smooth.
3. Fill each cupcake liner 2/3 full with the batter.
4. Bake for 18-20 minutes or until a toothpick inserted comes out clean.

5. Let the cupcakes cool completely.

6. Frost each cupcake with chocolate frosting.

7. Insert pretzel sticks into the cupcakes to resemble broomsticks.

8. Decorate with assorted Halloween candies to create a candy-coated look.

Summary: Candy-Coated Pretzel Cupcakes are a sweet and salty Halloween treat. The combination of chocolate cake, pretzel broomsticks, and candy toppings is delightful.

Tips and Tricks:

- You can use mini pretzel sticks for smaller broomsticks.

- Get creative with your choice of Halloween candies for decoration.

Vampire Bite Red Velvet Cupcakes

Ingredients:

- 1 box of red velvet cake mix
- 3 eggs
- 1/2 cup vegetable oil
- 1 cup buttermilk
- Red fruit preserves or raspberry jam
- Red velvet frosting
- Edible vampire bite decorations

Instructions:

1. Preheat your oven to 350°F (175°C) and line a cupcake pan with liners.
2. In a mixing bowl, combine the red velvet cake mix, eggs, vegetable oil, and buttermilk. Mix until smooth.
3. Fill each cupcake liner 2/3 full with the batter.
4. Bake for 18-20 minutes or until a toothpick inserted comes out clean.

5. Let the cupcakes cool completely.

6. Use a small spoon to create a hollow in the center of each cupcake.

7. Fill the hollow with red fruit preserves or raspberry jam to resemble a "vampire bite."

8. Frost the cupcakes with red velvet frosting.

9. Place edible vampire bite decorations on top.

Summary: Vampire Bite Red Velvet Cupcakes are a deliciously eerie Halloween treat. The "bite" in the center adds a spooky vampire touch.

Tips and Tricks:

- Adjust the amount of fruit preserves for your desired level of "blood."

- You can make your own vampire bite decorations with red fondant.

Monster Eyeball Cupcakes

Ingredients:

- 1 box of vanilla cake mix
- 3 eggs
- 1/2 cup vegetable oil
- 1 cup buttermilk
- Vanilla frosting
- Edible candy eyeballs
- Green gel food coloring

Instructions:

1. Preheat your oven to 350°F (175°C) and line a cupcake pan with liners.
2. In a mixing bowl, combine the vanilla cake mix, eggs, vegetable oil, and buttermilk. Mix until smooth.
3. Add a few drops of green gel food coloring to tint the batter green and mix until evenly colored.
4. Fill each cupcake liner 2/3 full with the batter.

5. Bake for 18-20 minutes or until a toothpick inserted comes out clean.

6. Let the cupcakes cool completely.

7. Frost each cupcake with vanilla frosting.

8. Place edible candy eyeballs on top to create a monster eyeball effect.

Summary: Monster Eyeball Cupcakes are a playful and visually striking Halloween treat. The candy eyeballs make them look like spooky monster eyes.

Tips and Tricks:

- Use different sizes of candy eyeballs for variety.
- You can experiment with different colors of frosting for a diverse monster-themed batch.

Haunted Graveyard Cupcakes

Ingredients:

- 1 box of chocolate cake mix
- 3 eggs
- 1/2 cup vegetable oil
- 1 cup water
- Chocolate frosting
- Crushed chocolate sandwich cookies (for "dirt")
- Edible tombstone decorations

Instructions:

1. Preheat your oven to 350°F (175°C) and line a cupcake pan with liners.
2. In a mixing bowl, combine the chocolate cake mix, eggs, vegetable oil, and water. Mix until smooth.
3. Fill each cupcake liner 2/3 full with the batter.
4. Bake for 18-20 minutes or until a toothpick inserted comes out clean.
5. Let the cupcakes cool completely.

6. Frost each cupcake with chocolate frosting.

7. Sprinkle crushed chocolate sandwich cookies on top to resemble "dirt."

8. Place edible tombstone decorations in the "graveyard."

Summary: Haunted Graveyard Cupcakes are a spooky and creative Halloween dessert. The edible tombstones atop "dirt" make them perfect for a haunted theme.

Tips and Tricks:

- You can use rectangular pieces of chocolate or fondant as tombstones.

- Arrange the tombstones in different angles for a more realistic graveyard look.

Witch's Brew Cupcakes

Ingredients:

- 1 box of green apple cake mix
- 3 eggs
- 1/2 cup vegetable oil
- 1 cup water
- Green apple frosting
- Gummy worms (for garnish)
- Edible cauldron decorations

Instructions:

1. Preheat your oven to 350°F (175°C) and line a cupcake pan with liners.
2. In a mixing bowl, combine the green apple cake mix, eggs, vegetable oil, and water. Mix until well combined.
3. Fill each cupcake liner 2/3 full with the batter.
4. Bake for 18-20 minutes or until a toothpick inserted comes out clean.

5. Let the cupcakes cool completely.

6. Frost each cupcake with green apple frosting.

7. Garnish with gummy worms to create a "witch's brew" look.

8. Place edible cauldron decorations on top for added witchy charm.

Summary: Witch's Brew Cupcakes are a whimsical and flavorful Halloween treat. The green apple flavor and spooky decorations make them perfect for a witch's cauldron theme.

Tips and Tricks:

- You can use crushed graham crackers as "dirt" before placing the cauldron decorations.

- Get creative with the positioning of the gummy worms for a playful effect.

Pumpkin Patch Chocolate Cupcakes

Ingredients:

- 1 box of chocolate cake mix
- 3 eggs
- 1/2 cup vegetable oil
- 1 cup water
- Chocolate frosting
- Pumpkin-shaped candies (e.g., Reese's Pieces)
- Crushed chocolate cookies (for "dirt")

Instructions:

1. Preheat your oven to 350°F (175°C) and line a cupcake pan with liners.
2. In a mixing bowl, combine the chocolate cake mix, eggs, vegetable oil, and water. Mix until smooth.
3. Fill each cupcake liner 2/3 full with the batter.
4. Bake for 18-20 minutes or until a toothpick inserted comes out clean.
5. Let the cupcakes cool completely.

6. Frost each cupcake with chocolate frosting.

7. Press pumpkin-shaped candies into the frosting to create a pumpkin patch.

8. Sprinkle crushed chocolate cookies around the pumpkins for a "dirt" effect.

Summary: Pumpkin Patch Chocolate Cupcakes are a delightful and festive Halloween treat. The pumpkin-shaped candies make them resemble a pumpkin patch.

Tips and Tricks:

- You can use orange frosting instead of chocolate for a pumpkin-themed color.

- Position the pumpkins creatively to mimic a real pumpkin patch.

Ghostly Peanut Butter Cup Cupcakes

Ingredients:

- 1 box of chocolate cake mix
- 3 eggs
- 1/2 cup vegetable oil
- 1 cup water
- Peanut butter frosting
- Mini peanut butter cups
- Edible ghost decorations

Instructions:

1. Preheat your oven to 350°F (175°C) and line a cupcake pan with liners.
2. In a mixing bowl, combine the chocolate cake mix, eggs, vegetable oil, and water. Mix until smooth.
3. Fill each cupcake liner 2/3 full with the batter.
4. Bake for 18-20 minutes or until a toothpick inserted comes out clean.
5. Let the cupcakes cool completely.

6. Frost each cupcake with peanut butter frosting.

7. Place mini peanut butter cups on top of each cupcake to create ghostly heads.

8. Position edible ghost decorations beside the peanut butter cups for a spooky touch.

Summary: Ghostly Peanut Butter Cup Cupcakes are a peanut butter lover's dream for Halloween. The mini peanut butter cup ghosts add a playful and tasty element.

Tips and Tricks:

- You can use different sizes of mini peanut butter cups for variety.

- Make sure the edible ghost decorations are securely placed.

Candy Corn Buttercream Cupcakes

Ingredients:

- 1 box of vanilla cake mix
- 3 eggs
- 1/2 cup vegetable oil
- 1 cup buttermilk
- Candy corn buttercream frosting
- Candy corn (for garnish)

Instructions:

1. Preheat your oven to 350°F (175°C) and line a cupcake pan with liners.
2. In a mixing bowl, combine the vanilla cake mix, eggs, vegetable oil, and buttermilk. Mix until smooth.
3. Fill each cupcake liner 2/3 full with the batter.
4. Bake for 18-20 minutes or until a toothpick inserted comes out clean.
5. Let the cupcakes cool completely.

6. Frost each cupcake with candy corn buttercream frosting.

7. Garnish with candy corn for a classic Halloween look.

Summary: Candy Corn Buttercream Cupcakes are a sweet and festive Halloween treat. The candy corn frosting and garnish add a pop of color and flavor.

Tips and Tricks:

- If you prefer a less sweet frosting, use a vanilla buttercream and add crushed candy corn to it.

- Arrange the candy corn in various patterns for a playful appearance.

Witches' Hat Chocolate Cupcakes

Ingredients:

- 1 box of chocolate cake mix
- 3 eggs
- 1/2 cup vegetable oil
- 1 cup water
- Chocolate frosting
- Chocolate wafer cookies
- Hershey's Kisses candies

Instructions:

1. Preheat your oven to 350°F (175°C) and line a cupcake pan with liners.
2. In a mixing bowl, combine the chocolate cake mix, eggs, vegetable oil, and water. Mix until smooth.
3. Fill each cupcake liner 2/3 full with the batter.
4. Bake for 18-20 minutes or until a toothpick inserted comes out clean.
5. Let the cupcakes cool completely.

6. Frost each cupcake with chocolate frosting.

7. For each cupcake, gently press a chocolate wafer cookie upside down onto the frosting.

8. Place a Hershey's Kiss on top of the wafer cookie to create a witches' hat.

Summary: Witches' Hat Chocolate Cupcakes are a whimsical and delicious Halloween treat. The chocolate wafer cookies and Hershey's Kisses form charming witches' hats.

Tips and Tricks:

- You can use colored frosting to add a ribbon around the base of the witches' hats.

- Ensure that the wafer cookies are firmly attached to the frosting.

Pumpkin Spice Latte Cupcakes

Ingredients:

- 1 box of pumpkin spice cake mix
- 3 eggs
- 1/2 cup vegetable oil
- 1 cup brewed coffee (cooled)
- Pumpkin spice frosting
- Cinnamon sticks (for garnish)

Instructions:

1. Preheat your oven to 350°F (175°C) and line a cupcake pan with liners.
2. In a mixing bowl, combine the pumpkin spice cake mix, eggs, vegetable oil, and brewed coffee. Mix until well combined.
3. Fill each cupcake liner 2/3 full with the batter.
4. Bake for 18-20 minutes or until a toothpick inserted comes out clean.
5. Let the cupcakes cool completely.

6. Frost each cupcake with pumpkin spice frosting.

7. Garnish with a small cinnamon stick on top for a latte-inspired touch.

Summary: Pumpkin Spice Latte Cupcakes are a delightful and cozy Halloween treat. The pumpkin spice and coffee flavors make them reminiscent of a latte.

Tips and Tricks:

- You can sprinkle a dash of ground cinnamon on top of the frosting for extra spice.

- Serve these cupcakes with a cup of coffee for the full latte experience.

Frankenstein's Monster Mint Cupcakes

Ingredients:

- 1 box of mint chocolate chip cake mix
- 3 eggs
- 1/2 cup vegetable oil
- 1 cup milk
- Mint chocolate frosting
- Edible Frankenstein face decorations

Instructions:

1. Preheat your oven to 350°F (175°C) and line a cupcake pan with liners.
2. In a mixing bowl, combine the mint chocolate chip cake mix, eggs, vegetable oil, and milk. Mix until well combined.
3. Fill each cupcake liner 2/3 full with the batter.
4. Bake for 18-20 minutes or until a toothpick inserted comes out clean.
5. Let the cupcakes cool completely.

6. Frost each cupcake with mint chocolate frosting.

7. Place edible Frankenstein face decorations on top to create a spooky monster look.

Summary: Frankenstein's Monster Mint Cupcakes are a minty and playful Halloween treat. The edible Frankenstein faces give them a spooky twist.

Tips and Tricks:

- You can make your own Frankenstein face decorations using colored fondant or purchase them from a baking supply store.
- Experiment with different expressions for the Frankenstein faces.

Spider's Nest Chocolate Cupcakes

Ingredients:

- 1 box of chocolate cake mix
- 3 eggs
- 1/2 cup vegetable oil
- 1 cup water
- Chocolate frosting
- Chocolate vermicelli (for spider nests)
- Plastic spiders (for garnish)

Instructions:

1. Preheat your oven to 350°F (175°C) and line a cupcake pan with liners.
2. In a mixing bowl, combine the chocolate cake mix, eggs, vegetable oil, and water. Mix until smooth.
3. Fill each cupcake liner 2/3 full with the batter.
4. Bake for 18-20 minutes or until a toothpick inserted comes out clean.
5. Let the cupcakes cool completely.

6. Frost each cupcake with chocolate frosting.

7. Sprinkle chocolate vermicelli on top to create spider nests.

8. Place plastic spiders on the nests for a creepy-crawly effect.

Summary: Spider's Nest Chocolate Cupcakes are a spooky and fun Halloween treat. The chocolate vermicelli and plastic spiders make them resemble spider nests.

Tips and Tricks:

- You can use black licorice strings as spider legs for added realism.

- Position the plastic spiders strategically to enhance the creepy effect.

Caramel Apple Cupcakes

Ingredients:

- 1 box of apple spice cake mix
- 3 eggs
- 1/2 cup vegetable oil
- 1 cup buttermilk
- Caramel frosting
- Caramel sauce (for drizzling)
- Sliced apples (for garnish)

Instructions:

1. Preheat your oven to 350°F (175°C) and line a cupcake pan with liners.
2. In a mixing bowl, combine the apple spice cake mix, eggs, vegetable oil, and buttermilk. Mix until well combined.
3. Fill each cupcake liner 2/3 full with the batter.
4. Bake for 18-20 minutes or until a toothpick inserted comes out clean.

5. Let the cupcakes cool completely.

6. Frost each cupcake with caramel frosting.

7. Drizzle caramel sauce on top of each cupcake.

8. Garnish with a slice of apple for a caramel apple-inspired look.

Summary: Caramel Apple Cupcakes are a sweet and autumn-inspired Halloween treat. The combination of apple spice and caramel is irresistible.

Tips and Tricks:

- You can sprinkle a pinch of cinnamon on top for extra flavor.

- Dip the apple slices in lemon juice to prevent browning.

Eyeball Pudding-Filled Cupcakes

Ingredients:

- 1 box of chocolate cake mix
- 3 eggs
- 1/2 cup vegetable oil
- 1 cup water
- Chocolate frosting
- Chocolate pudding cups
- Edible candy eyeballs

Instructions:

1. Preheat your oven to 350°F (175°C) and line a cupcake pan with liners.
2. In a mixing bowl, combine the chocolate cake mix, eggs, vegetable oil, and water. Mix until smooth.
3. Fill each cupcake liner 2/3 full with the batter.
4. Bake for 18-20 minutes or until a toothpick inserted comes out clean.
5. Let the cupcakes cool completely.

6. Frost each cupcake with chocolate frosting.

7. Carefully remove the tops of the chocolate pudding cups.

8. Place a pudding cup upside down in the center of each cupcake.

9. Press edible candy eyeballs into the pudding to create spooky eyeball cupcakes.

Summary: Eyeball Pudding-Filled Cupcakes are a playful and gooey Halloween treat. The surprise pudding filling and candy eyeballs make them delightfully creepy.

Tips and Tricks:

- Use a sharp knife to remove the tops of the pudding cups.
- You can experiment with different pudding flavors for variety.

Black Cat Chocolate Cupcakes

Ingredients:

- 1 box of chocolate cake mix
- 3 eggs
- 1/2 cup vegetable oil
- 1 cup water
- Chocolate frosting
- Black licorice (for cat tails)
- Edible cat face decorations

Instructions:

1. Preheat your oven to 350°F (175°C) and line a cupcake pan with liners.
2. In a mixing bowl, combine the chocolate cake mix, eggs, vegetable oil, and water. Mix until smooth.
3. Fill each cupcake liner 2/3 full with the batter.
4. Bake for 18-20 minutes or until a toothpick inserted comes out clean.
5. Let the cupcakes cool completely.

6. Frost each cupcake with chocolate frosting.

7. Cut small pieces of black licorice for cat tails and insert them into the cupcakes.

8. Place edible cat face decorations on top for a cute black cat look.

Summary: Black Cat Chocolate Cupcakes are an adorable and Halloween-themed treat. The licorice tails and edible cat faces make them resemble black cats.

Tips and Tricks:

- You can use candy-coated chocolate pieces for the cat eyes.

- Ensure that the licorice tails are firmly inserted into the cupcakes.

Jack-o'-Lantern Pumpkin Cupcakes

Ingredients:

- 1 box of pumpkin spice cake mix
- 3 eggs
- 1/2 cup vegetable oil
- 1 cup water
- Cream cheese frosting
- Orange food coloring
- Black decorating gel

Instructions:

1. Preheat your oven to 350°F (175°C) and line a cupcake pan with liners.
2. In a mixing bowl, combine the pumpkin spice cake mix, eggs, vegetable oil, and water. Mix until well combined.
3. Fill each cupcake liner 2/3 full with the batter.
4. Bake for 18-20 minutes or until a toothpick inserted comes out clean.

5. Let the cupcakes cool completely.

6. Tint the cream cheese frosting with orange food coloring until you achieve the desired pumpkin color.

7. Frost each cupcake with the orange frosting.

8. Use black decorating gel to draw jack-o'-lantern faces on top of the cupcakes.

Summary: Jack-o'-Lantern Pumpkin Cupcakes are a classic and festive Halloween treat. The jack-o'-lantern faces add a fun and spooky touch.

Tips and Tricks:

- Experiment with different facial expressions for the jack-o'-lanterns.

- You can also use mini chocolate chips for the eyes and mouth.

Zombie Brain Raspberry Cupcakes

Ingredients:

- 1 box of raspberry-flavored cake mix
- 3 eggs
- 1/2 cup vegetable oil
- 1 cup buttermilk
- Raspberry frosting
- Red gel food coloring
- Edible zombie brain decorations

Instructions:

1. Preheat your oven to 350°F (175°C) and line a cupcake pan with liners.
2. In a mixing bowl, combine the raspberry-flavored cake mix, eggs, vegetable oil, and buttermilk. Mix until well combined.
3. Fill each cupcake liner 2/3 full with the batter.
4. Bake for 18-20 minutes or until a toothpick inserted comes out clean.

5. Let the cupcakes cool completely.

6. Tint the raspberry frosting with red gel food coloring until you achieve a deep red color.

7. Frost each cupcake with the red frosting.

8. Place edible zombie brain decorations on top for a creepy zombie theme.

Summary: Zombie Brain Raspberry Cupcakes are a gory and spooky Halloween treat. The raspberry flavor and edible brains create a chilling effect.

Tips and Tricks:

- You can use white frosting as a base for the brains and add red gel to create a bloody appearance.

- Arrange the edible brains in different positions for variety.

Haunted Castle Cookie Cupcakes

Ingredients:

- 1 box of vanilla cake mix
- 3 eggs
- 1/2 cup vegetable oil
- 1 cup buttermilk
- Vanilla frosting
- Halloween castle cookie decorations

Instructions:

1. Preheat your oven to 350°F (175°C) and line a cupcake pan with liners.
2. In a mixing bowl, combine the vanilla cake mix, eggs, vegetable oil, and buttermilk. Mix until smooth.
3. Fill each cupcake liner 2/3 full with the batter.
4. Bake for 18-20 minutes or until a toothpick inserted comes out clean.
5. Let the cupcakes cool completely.

6. Frost each cupcake with vanilla frosting.

7. Place Halloween castle cookie decorations on top for a haunted castle theme.

Summary: Haunted Castle Cookie Cupcakes are a whimsical and Halloween-inspired treat. The castle cookie decorations make them look like spooky haunted castles.

Tips and Tricks:

- You can add edible glitter or colored sugar for a magical touch.

- Arrange the castle cookies creatively to create a castle landscape.

Midnight Pumpkin Cupcakes

Ingredients:

- 1 box of chocolate cake mix
- 3 eggs
- 1/2 cup vegetable oil
- 1 cup buttermilk
- Pumpkin-shaped sprinkles
- Black icing gel

Instructions:

1. Preheat your oven to 350°F (175°C) and line a cupcake pan with liners.
2. In a mixing bowl, combine the chocolate cake mix, eggs, vegetable oil, and buttermilk. Mix until smooth.
3. Fill each cupcake liner 2/3 full with the batter.
4. Bake for 18-20 minutes or until a toothpick inserted comes out clean.
5. Let the cupcakes cool completely.

6. Frost each cupcake with black icing gel to create a midnight sky.

7. Sprinkle pumpkin-shaped sprinkles on top for a spooky pumpkin patch look.

Summary: Midnight Pumpkin Cupcakes are a simple and festive Halloween treat. The black icing gel and pumpkin-shaped sprinkles create a spooky atmosphere.

Tips and Tricks:

- You can use orange or green frosting for additional Halloween colors.

- Get creative with your pumpkin patch design.

Witch's Cauldron Chocolate Cupcakes

Ingredients:

- 1 box of chocolate cake mix
- 3 eggs
- 1/2 cup vegetable oil
- 1 cup water
- Green frosting
- Black licorice (for cauldron handles)
- Edible cauldron decorations

Instructions:

1. Preheat your oven to 350°F (175°C) and line a cupcake pan with liners.
2. In a mixing bowl, combine the chocolate cake mix, eggs, vegetable oil, and water. Mix until smooth.
3. Fill each cupcake liner 2/3 full with the batter.
4. Bake for 18-20 minutes or until a toothpick inserted comes out clean.
5. Let the cupcakes cool completely.

6. Frost each cupcake with green frosting.

7. Attach pieces of black licorice as cauldron handles to the sides of each cupcake.

8. Place edible cauldron decorations on top for a witch's cauldron theme.

Summary: Witch's Cauldron Chocolate Cupcakes are a whimsical and Halloween-inspired treat. The licorice handles and cauldron decorations make them look like bubbling cauldrons.

Tips and Tricks:

- Use different shapes of edible cauldron decorations for variety.

- Ensure the licorice handles are securely attached.

Spiderweb White Chocolate Cupcakes

Ingredients:

- 1 box of white chocolate cake mix
- 3 eggs
- 1/2 cup vegetable oil
- 1 cup milk
- White frosting
- Black icing gel
- Plastic spiders (for garnish)

Instructions:

1. Preheat your oven to 350°F (175°C) and line a cupcake pan with liners.
2. In a mixing bowl, combine the white chocolate cake mix, eggs, vegetable oil, and milk. Mix until well combined.
3. Fill each cupcake liner 2/3 full with the batter.
4. Bake for 18-20 minutes or until a toothpick inserted comes out clean.

5. Let the cupcakes cool completely.
6. Frost each cupcake with white frosting.
7. Use black icing gel to draw spiderweb designs on top of the frosting.
8. Place plastic spiders on the webs for a spooky spiderweb look.

Summary: Spiderweb White Chocolate Cupcakes are a creepy and elegant Halloween treat. The spiderweb designs and plastic spiders create a spooky atmosphere.

Tips and Tricks:

- Practice drawing spiderwebs on parchment paper before decorating the cupcakes.
- Arrange the plastic spiders in different positions for variety.

Candy Corn Vanilla Cupcakes

Ingredients:

- 1 box of vanilla cake mix
- 3 eggs
- 1/2 cup vegetable oil
- 1 cup buttermilk
- Vanilla frosting
- Candy corn (for garnish)

Instructions:

1. Preheat your oven to 350°F (175°C) and line a cupcake pan with liners.
2. In a mixing bowl, combine the vanilla cake mix, eggs, vegetable oil, and buttermilk. Mix until smooth.
3. Fill each cupcake liner 2/3 full with the batter.
4. Bake for 18-20 minutes or until a toothpick inserted comes out clean.
5. Let the cupcakes cool completely.

6. Frost each cupcake with vanilla frosting.

7. Garnish with candy corn for a classic Halloween look.

Summary: Candy Corn Vanilla Cupcakes are a sweet and colorful Halloween treat. The candy corn garnish adds a pop of Halloween colors.

Tips and Tricks:

- Use candy corn in different patterns for a playful appearance.

- You can add a touch of orange food coloring to the frosting for an extra burst of color.

Bloody Vampire Bite Cupcakes

Ingredients:

- 1 box of red velvet cake mix
- 3 eggs
- 1/2 cup vegetable oil
- 1 cup buttermilk
- Red velvet frosting
- Edible vampire bite decorations
- Red food coloring (optional)

Instructions:

1. Preheat your oven to 350°F (175°C) and line a cupcake pan with liners.

2. In a mixing bowl, combine the red velvet cake mix, eggs, vegetable oil, and buttermilk. Mix until well combined.

3. Fill each cupcake liner 2/3 full with the batter.

4. Bake for 18-20 minutes or until a toothpick inserted comes out clean.

5. Let the cupcakes cool completely.

6. Frost each cupcake with red velvet frosting.

7. Place edible vampire bite decorations on top to create a spooky vampire bite look.

8. If desired, add a few drops of red food coloring to the frosting for a deeper red hue.

Summary: Bloody Vampire Bite Cupcakes are a chilling and delicious Halloween treat. The vampire bite decorations and red velvet flavor add a spooky touch.

Tips and Tricks:

- Adjust the amount of red food coloring for your desired blood-red color.

- Position the vampire bite decorations strategically for realism.

Ghostly Marshmallow Cupcakes

Ingredients:

- 1 box of vanilla cake mix
- 3 eggs
- 1/2 cup vegetable oil
- 1 cup buttermilk
- Marshmallow frosting
- Edible ghost decorations

Instructions:

1. Preheat your oven to 350°F (175°C) and line a cupcake pan with liners.
2. In a mixing bowl, combine the vanilla cake mix, eggs, vegetable oil, and buttermilk. Mix until smooth.
3. Fill each cupcake liner 2/3 full with the batter.
4. Bake for 18-20 minutes or until a toothpick inserted comes out clean.
5. Let the cupcakes cool completely.

6. Frost each cupcake with marshmallow frosting.

7. Place edible ghost decorations on top for a ghostly appearance.

Summary: Ghostly Marshmallow Cupcakes are a cute and ghost-themed Halloween treat. The marshmallow frosting and edible ghosts make them playful and spooky.

Tips and Tricks:

- You can use black icing gel to add ghostly eyes and mouths for extra detail.

- Get creative with the positioning of the ghost decorations.

Mummy Wrapped Banana Cupcakes

Ingredients:

- 1 box of banana cake mix
- 3 eggs
- 1/2 cup vegetable oil
- 1 cup mashed bananas
- Cream cheese frosting
- Edible candy eyes
- White fondant (for mummy wraps)

Instructions:

1. Preheat your oven to 350°F (175°C) and line a cupcake pan with liners.
2. In a mixing bowl, combine the banana cake mix, eggs, vegetable oil, and mashed bananas. Mix until well combined.
3. Fill each cupcake liner 2/3 full with the batter.
4. Bake for 18-20 minutes or until a toothpick inserted comes out clean.

5. Let the cupcakes cool completely.

6. Frost each cupcake with cream cheese frosting.

7. Use strips of white fondant to wrap around each cupcake like mummy bandages.

8. Place edible candy eyes on top for mummy eyes.

Summary: Mummy Wrapped Banana Cupcakes are a delightful and mummy-themed Halloween treat. The fondant wraps and candy eyes make them resemble cute mummies.

Tips and Tricks:

- Roll out the fondant strips thinly for a realistic mummy appearance.

- Experiment with different expressions for the mummy eyes.

Poison Apple Caramel Cupcakes

Ingredients:

- 1 box of caramel apple cake mix
- 3 eggs
- 1/2 cup vegetable oil
- 1 cup buttermilk
- Caramel frosting
- Edible poison apple decorations
- Caramel sauce (for drizzling)

Instructions:

1. Preheat your oven to 350°F (175°C) and line a cupcake pan with liners.
2. In a mixing bowl, combine the caramel apple cake mix, eggs, vegetable oil, and buttermilk. Mix until well combined.
3. Fill each cupcake liner 2/3 full with the batter.
4. Bake for 18-20 minutes or until a toothpick inserted comes out clean.

5. Let the cupcakes cool completely.

6. Frost each cupcake with caramel frosting.

7. Place edible poison apple decorations on top for a wickedly delicious look.

8. Drizzle caramel sauce over the cupcakes for added flavor.

Summary: Poison Apple Caramel Cupcakes are a tempting and Halloween-inspired treat. The caramel apple flavor and poison apple decorations add a touch of evil magic.

Tips and Tricks:

- Warm the caramel sauce slightly before drizzling for easier application.

- Position the poison apple decorations creatively for a mysterious effect.

Bat Chocolate Cherry Cupcakes

Ingredients:

- 1 box of chocolate cherry cake mix
- 3 eggs
- 1/2 cup vegetable oil
- 1 cup water
- Chocolate frosting
- Edible bat decorations

Instructions:

1. Preheat your oven to 350°F (175°C) and line a cupcake pan with liners.
2. In a mixing bowl, combine the chocolate cherry cake mix, eggs, vegetable oil, and water. Mix until smooth.
3. Fill each cupcake liner 2/3 full with the batter.
4. Bake for 18-20 minutes or until a toothpick inserted comes out clean.
5. Let the cupcakes cool completely.

6. Frost each cupcake with chocolate frosting.

7. Place edible bat decorations on top for a spooky bat-themed look.

Summary: Bat Chocolate Cherry Cupcakes are a flavorful and Halloween-themed treat. The chocolate cherry flavor and bat decorations create a mysterious atmosphere.

Tips and Tricks:

- You can use black icing gel to add details to the bat decorations.

- Get creative with the positioning of the bat decorations for a dynamic look.

Skeleton Bone Vanilla Cupcakes

Ingredients:

- 1 box of vanilla cake mix
- 3 eggs
- 1/2 cup vegetable oil
- 1 cup buttermilk
- Vanilla frosting
- Edible skeleton bone decorations

Instructions:

1. Preheat your oven to 350°F (175°C) and line a cupcake pan with liners.
2. In a mixing bowl, combine the vanilla cake mix, eggs, vegetable oil, and buttermilk. Mix until smooth.
3. Fill each cupcake liner 2/3 full with the batter.
4. Bake for 18-20 minutes or until a toothpick inserted comes out clean.
5. Let the cupcakes cool completely.

6. Frost each cupcake with vanilla frosting.

7. Place edible skeleton bone decorations on top for a spooky skeleton theme.

Summary: Skeleton Bone Vanilla Cupcakes are a fun and Halloween-themed treat. The edible skeleton bones add a playful and spooky touch.

Tips and Tricks:

- Use black icing gel to draw a skeleton face on some of the cupcakes for variety.

- Arrange the skeleton bones creatively for different poses.

Pumpkin Patch Cream Cheese Cupcakes

Ingredients:

- 1 box of pumpkin spice cake mix
- 3 eggs
- 1/2 cup vegetable oil
- 1 cup buttermilk
- Cream cheese frosting
- Edible pumpkin decorations
- Crushed graham crackers (for "dirt")

Instructions:

1. Preheat your oven to 350°F (175°C) and line a cupcake pan with liners.
2. In a mixing bowl, combine the pumpkin spice cake mix, eggs, vegetable oil, and buttermilk. Mix until well combined.
3. Fill each cupcake liner 2/3 full with the batter.

4. Bake for 18-20 minutes or until a toothpick inserted comes out clean.

5. Let the cupcakes cool completely.

6. Frost each cupcake with cream cheese frosting.

7. Place edible pumpkin decorations on top to create a pumpkin patch.

8. Sprinkle crushed graham crackers around the pumpkins for a "dirt" effect.

Summary: Pumpkin Patch Cream Cheese Cupcakes are a delightful and festive Halloween treat. The pumpkin decorations and "dirt" make them resemble a pumpkin patch.

Tips and Tricks:

- You can use orange frosting instead of cream cheese for a pumpkin-themed color.

- Position the pumpkins creatively to mimic a real pumpkin patch.

Slime-Filled Alien Cupcakes

Ingredients:

- 1 box of green alien slime cake mix
- 3 eggs
- 1/2 cup vegetable oil
- 1 cup milk
- Green frosting
- Edible alien decorations
- Green gel food coloring (optional)

Instructions:

1. Preheat your oven to 350°F (175°C) and line a cupcake pan with liners.
2. In a mixing bowl, combine the green alien slime cake mix, eggs, vegetable oil, and milk. Mix until well combined.
3. Fill each cupcake liner 2/3 full with the batter.
4. Bake for 18-20 minutes or until a toothpick inserted comes out clean.

5. Let the cupcakes cool completely.

6. Frost each cupcake with green frosting.

7. Place edible alien decorations on top for a slimy alien look.

8. If desired, add a few drops of green gel food coloring to the frosting for a vibrant green color.

Summary: Slime-Filled Alien Cupcakes are a playful and extraterrestrial Halloween treat. The green color and alien decorations create an otherworldly atmosphere.

Tips and Tricks:

- Adjust the amount of green food coloring for your preferred shade of green.

- Get creative with the positioning of the alien decorations for an alien invasion theme.

Gory Brain Chocolate Cupcakes

Ingredients:

- 1 box of chocolate brain cake mix
- 3 eggs
- 1/2 cup vegetable oil
- 1 cup buttermilk
- Chocolate frosting
- Edible brain decorations
- Red gel food coloring

Instructions:

1. Preheat your oven to 350°F (175°C) and line a cupcake pan with liners.
2. In a mixing bowl, combine the chocolate brain cake mix, eggs, vegetable oil, and buttermilk. Mix until smooth.
3. Fill each cupcake liner 2/3 full with the batter.
4. Bake for 18-20 minutes or until a toothpick inserted comes out clean.

5. Let the cupcakes cool completely.

6. Frost each cupcake with chocolate frosting.

7. Place edible brain decorations on top for a gory brain theme.

8. Add red gel food coloring to create a "bloody" effect on the brains.

Summary: Gory Brain Chocolate Cupcakes are a gruesome and delicious Halloween treat. The edible brain decorations and "blood" add a horrifying touch.

Tips and Tricks:

- Be cautious with the red gel food coloring, as a little goes a long way.

- Position the brain decorations creatively for a creepy appearance.

Creepy Crawler Oreo Cupcakes

Ingredients:

- 1 box of cookies and cream cake mix
- 3 eggs
- 1/2 cup vegetable oil
- 1 cup milk
- Oreo frosting
- Gummy worms (for garnish)
- Crushed Oreo cookies (for topping)

Instructions:

1. Preheat your oven to 350°F (175°C) and line a cupcake pan with liners.
2. In a mixing bowl, combine the cookies and cream cake mix, eggs, vegetable oil, and milk. Mix until well combined.
3. Fill each cupcake liner 2/3 full with the batter.
4. Bake for 18-20 minutes or until a toothpick inserted comes out clean.

5. Let the cupcakes cool completely.

6. Frost each cupcake with Oreo frosting.

7. Garnish with gummy worms crawling out of the frosting.

8. Sprinkle crushed Oreo cookies on top for added texture and flavor.

Summary: Creepy Crawler Oreo Cupcakes are a fun and creepy Halloween treat. The gummy worms and crushed Oreos create a spooky and delicious combination.

Tips and Tricks:

- You can use different types of Oreo cookies for variety.

- Position the gummy worms to make them look like they are crawling out of the cupcakes.

Wicked Witch Potion Cupcakes

Ingredients:

- 1 box of black potion cake mix
- 3 eggs
- 1/2 cup vegetable oil
- 1 cup buttermilk
- Witch hat decorations
- Edible potion bottle decorations
- Black frosting

Instructions:

1. Preheat your oven to 350°F (175°C) and line a cupcake pan with liners.
2. In a mixing bowl, combine the black potion cake mix, eggs, vegetable oil, and buttermilk. Mix until smooth.
3. Fill each cupcake liner 2/3 full with the batter.
4. Bake for 18-20 minutes or until a toothpick inserted comes out clean.

5. Let the cupcakes cool completely.

6. Frost each cupcake with black frosting.

7. Place witch hat and potion bottle decorations on top for a wicked witch theme.

Summary: Wicked Witch Potion Cupcakes are a dark and enchanting Halloween treat. The witch hat and potion bottle decorations add a magical touch.

Tips and Tricks:

- Position the decorations creatively to create a spellbinding scene.

- You can use silver or gold edible paint to add details to the potion bottles.

Haunted House Chocolate Cupcakes

Ingredients:

- 1 box of chocolate cake mix
- 3 eggs
- 1/2 cup vegetable oil
- 1 cup buttermilk
- Chocolate frosting
- Edible haunted house decorations

Instructions:

1. Preheat your oven to 350°F (175°C) and line a cupcake pan with liners.
2. In a mixing bowl, combine the chocolate cake mix, eggs, vegetable oil, and buttermilk. Mix until smooth.
3. Fill each cupcake liner 2/3 full with the batter.
4. Bake for 18-20 minutes or until a toothpick inserted comes out clean.
5. Let the cupcakes cool completely.

6. Frost each cupcake with chocolate frosting.

7. Place edible haunted house decorations on top for a spooky haunted house theme.

Summary: Haunted House Chocolate Cupcakes are a spooky and Halloween-themed treat. The haunted house decorations create a mysterious and eerie atmosphere.

Tips and Tricks:

- You can use black icing gel to add details to the haunted house decorations.

- Position the haunted houses creatively for a hauntingly beautiful scene.

Pumpkin Spice Latte Cupcakes

Ingredients:

- 1 box of pumpkin spice cake mix
- 3 eggs
- 1/2 cup vegetable oil
- 1 cup brewed coffee (cooled)
- Pumpkin spice frosting
- Cinnamon sticks (for garnish)

Instructions:

1. Preheat your oven to 350°F (175°C) and line a cupcake pan with liners.
2. In a mixing bowl, combine the pumpkin spice cake mix, eggs, vegetable oil, and brewed coffee. Mix until well combined.
3. Fill each cupcake liner 2/3 full with the batter.
4. Bake for 18-20 minutes or until a toothpick inserted comes out clean.
5. Let the cupcakes cool completely.

6. Frost each cupcake with pumpkin spice frosting.

7. Garnish with a small cinnamon stick on top for a latte-inspired touch.

Summary: Pumpkin Spice Latte Cupcakes are a delightful and cozy Halloween treat. The pumpkin spice and coffee flavors make them reminiscent of a latte.

Tips and Tricks:

- You can sprinkle a dash of ground cinnamon on top of the frosting for extra spice.

- Serve these cupcakes with a cup of coffee for the full latte experience.

Frankenstein's Monster Mint Cupcakes

Ingredients:

- 1 box of mint chocolate chip cake mix
- 3 eggs
- 1/2 cup vegetable oil
- 1 cup milk
- Mint chocolate frosting
- Edible Frankenstein face decorations

Instructions:

1. Preheat your oven to 350°F (175°C) and line a cupcake pan with liners.
2. In a mixing bowl, combine the mint chocolate chip cake mix, eggs, vegetable oil, and milk. Mix until well combined.
3. Fill each cupcake liner 2/3 full with the batter.
4. Bake for 18-20 minutes or until a toothpick inserted comes out clean.
5. Let the cupcakes cool completely.

6. Frost each cupcake with mint chocolate frosting.

7. Place edible Frankenstein face decorations on top for a monstrous Frankenstein look.

Summary: Frankenstein's Monster Mint Cupcakes are a spooky and minty Halloween treat. The Frankenstein face decorations add a fun and eerie touch.

Tips and Tricks:

- Use black icing gel to add extra details to the Frankenstein faces.

- Experiment with different expressions for the monsters.

Swamp Creature Green Tea Cupcakes

Ingredients:

- 1 box of green tea matcha cake mix
- 3 eggs
- 1/2 cup vegetable oil
- 1 cup milk
- Green tea frosting
- Edible swamp creature decorations

Instructions:

1. Preheat your oven to 350°F (175°C) and line a cupcake pan with liners.
2. In a mixing bowl, combine the green tea matcha cake mix, eggs, vegetable oil, and milk. Mix until well combined.
3. Fill each cupcake liner 2/3 full with the batter.
4. Bake for 18-20 minutes or until a toothpick inserted comes out clean.
5. Let the cupcakes cool completely.

6. Frost each cupcake with green tea frosting.

7. Place edible swamp creature decorations on top for a swampy and mysterious look.

Summary: Swamp Creature Green Tea Cupcakes are an exotic and Halloween-themed treat. The green tea flavor and swamp creature decorations create a mystical atmosphere.

Tips and Tricks:

- Experiment with different swamp creature decorations for variety.

- You can add a drop of green food coloring to the frosting for a brighter green color.

Candy Apple Cinnamon Cupcakes

Ingredients:

- 1 box of cinnamon apple cake mix
- 3 eggs
- 1/2 cup vegetable oil
- 1 cup buttermilk
- Cinnamon frosting
- Mini candy apple decorations

Instructions:

1. Preheat your oven to 350°F (175°C) and line a cupcake pan with liners.
2. In a mixing bowl, combine the cinnamon apple cake mix, eggs, vegetable oil, and buttermilk. Mix until well combined.
3. Fill each cupcake liner 2/3 full with the batter.
4. Bake for 18-20 minutes or until a toothpick inserted comes out clean.
5. Let the cupcakes cool completely.

6. Frost each cupcake with cinnamon frosting.

7. Place mini candy apple decorations on top for a sweet and festive look.

Summary: Candy Apple Cinnamon Cupcakes are a delicious and fall-inspired Halloween treat. The cinnamon flavor and candy apple decorations make them reminiscent of autumn.

Tips and Tricks:

- You can drizzle caramel sauce over the frosting for an extra candy apple touch.

- Position the mini candy apples creatively for a charming appearance.

Spooky Eyeball Red Velvet Cupcakes

Ingredients:

- 1 box of red velvet cake mix
- 3 eggs
- 1/2 cup vegetable oil
- 1 cup buttermilk
- Red velvet frosting
- Edible eyeball decorations

Instructions:

1. Preheat your oven to 350°F (175°C) and line a cupcake pan with liners.
2. In a mixing bowl, combine the red velvet cake mix, eggs, vegetable oil, and buttermilk. Mix until smooth.
3. Fill each cupcake liner 2/3 full with the batter.
4. Bake for 18-20 minutes or until a toothpick inserted comes out clean.
5. Let the cupcakes cool completely.

6. Frost each cupcake with red velvet frosting.

7. Place edible eyeball decorations on top for a spooky eyeball theme.

Summary: Spooky Eyeball Red Velvet Cupcakes are a creepy and delicious Halloween treat. The edible eyeball decorations add a chilling touch.

Tips and Tricks:

- Use different sizes of edible eyeball decorations for variety.

- Create a bloodshot effect with red icing gel for extra spookiness.

Witch's Broomstick Chocolate Cupcakes

Ingredients:

- 1 box of chocolate cake mix
- 3 eggs
- 1/2 cup vegetable oil
- 1 cup buttermilk
- Chocolate frosting
- Pretzel sticks (for broomsticks)
- Edible witch's hat decorations

Instructions:

1. Preheat your oven to 350°F (175°C) and line a cupcake pan with liners.
2. In a mixing bowl, combine the chocolate cake mix, eggs, vegetable oil, and buttermilk. Mix until smooth.
3. Fill each cupcake liner 2/3 full with the batter.
4. Bake for 18-20 minutes or until a toothpick inserted comes out clean.

5. Let the cupcakes cool completely.

6. Frost each cupcake with chocolate frosting.

7. Insert a pretzel stick into each cupcake as a broomstick.

8. Place edible witch's hat decorations on top for a witch's broomstick look.

Summary: Witch's Broomstick Chocolate Cupcakes are a whimsical and Halloween-themed treat. The pretzel broomsticks and witch's hats create a playful and witchy atmosphere.

Tips and Tricks:

- Use pretzel sticks with salt for added flavor.
- Secure the pretzel sticks in the cupcakes by pushing them in at an angle.

Caramel Apple Streusel Cupcakes

Ingredients:

- 1 box of caramel apple cake mix
- 3 eggs
- 1/2 cup vegetable oil
- 1 cup buttermilk
- Caramel frosting
- Streusel topping (brown sugar, flour, butter, cinnamon)
- Mini caramel apple decorations

Instructions:

1. Preheat your oven to 350°F (175°C) and line a cupcake pan with liners.
2. In a mixing bowl, combine the caramel apple cake mix, eggs, vegetable oil, and buttermilk. Mix until well combined.
3. Fill each cupcake liner 2/3 full with the batter.

4. In a separate bowl, prepare the streusel topping by mixing brown sugar, flour, butter, and cinnamon until crumbly.

5. Sprinkle the streusel topping over the cupcake batter.

6. Bake for 18-20 minutes or until a toothpick inserted comes out clean.

7. Let the cupcakes cool completely.

8. Frost each cupcake with caramel frosting.

9. Garnish with mini caramel apple decorations for a delightful touch.

Summary: Caramel Apple Streusel Cupcakes are a sweet and autumn-inspired Halloween treat. The streusel topping and mini caramel apples add a crunchy and flavorful element.

Tips and Tricks:

- Make the streusel topping in advance for easy assembly.
- You can drizzle extra caramel sauce over the frosting for added caramel flavor.

Melted Witch Chocolate Cupcakes

Ingredients:

- 1 box of chocolate cake mix
- 3 eggs
- 1/2 cup vegetable oil
- 1 cup buttermilk
- Green frosting
- Edible witch leg decorations

Instructions:

1. Preheat your oven to 350°F (175°C) and line a cupcake pan with liners.
2. In a mixing bowl, combine the chocolate cake mix, eggs, vegetable oil, and buttermilk. Mix until smooth.
3. Fill each cupcake liner 2/3 full with the batter.
4. Bake for 18-20 minutes or until a toothpick inserted comes out clean.
5. Let the cupcakes cool completely.

6. Frost each cupcake with green frosting.

7. Place edible witch leg decorations on top for a melted witch theme.

Summary: Melted Witch Chocolate Cupcakes are a whimsical and Halloween-themed treat. The melted witch legs create a playful and spooky atmosphere.

Tips and Tricks:

- Use black icing gel to add details to the witch legs.
- Position the witch legs creatively for a hilarious effect.

Pumpkin Pie Spice Cupcakes

Ingredients:

- 1 box of pumpkin pie spice cake mix
- 3 eggs
- 1/2 cup vegetable oil
- 1 cup buttermilk
- Cream cheese frosting
- Pumpkin-shaped sprinkles
- Ground cinnamon (for garnish)

Instructions:

1. Preheat your oven to 350°F (175°C) and line a cupcake pan with liners.
2. In a mixing bowl, combine the pumpkin pie spice cake mix, eggs, vegetable oil, and buttermilk. Mix until well combined.
3. Fill each cupcake liner 2/3 full with the batter.
4. Bake for 18-20 minutes or until a toothpick inserted comes out clean.

5. Let the cupcakes cool completely.

6. Frost each cupcake with cream cheese frosting.

7. Sprinkle pumpkin-shaped sprinkles on top for a festive touch.

8. Dust with a pinch of ground cinnamon for extra flavor.

Summary: Pumpkin Pie Spice Cupcakes are a warm and cozy Halloween treat. The pumpkin spice and cream cheese frosting create a delightful fall flavor.

Tips and Tricks:

- You can use a piping bag to add a decorative swirl of frosting.

- Arrange the pumpkin-shaped sprinkles creatively for a charming appearance.

Creepy Crawly Spiderweb Cupcakes

Ingredients:

- 1 box of chocolate cake mix
- 3 eggs
- 1/2 cup vegetable oil
- 1 cup buttermilk
- Chocolate frosting
- Black icing gel
- Edible spider decorations

Instructions:

1. Preheat your oven to 350°F (175°C) and line a cupcake pan with liners.
2. In a mixing bowl, combine the chocolate cake mix, eggs, vegetable oil, and buttermilk. Mix until smooth.
3. Fill each cupcake liner 2/3 full with the batter.
4. Bake for 18-20 minutes or until a toothpick inserted comes out clean.

5. Let the cupcakes cool completely.

6. Frost each cupcake with chocolate frosting.

7. Use black icing gel to create a spiderweb design on top of each cupcake.

8. Place edible spider decorations on the webs for a creepy crawly look.

Summary: Creepy Crawly Spiderweb Cupcakes are a spooky and Halloween-themed treat. The spiderweb design and edible spiders add a chilling touch.

Tips and Tricks:

- Practice the spiderweb design on a piece of parchment paper before applying it to the cupcakes.

- Position the edible spiders creatively for a spooky scene.

Monster Mash Banana Cupcakes

Ingredients:

- 1 box of banana cake mix
- 3 eggs
- 1/2 cup vegetable oil
- 1 cup mashed bananas
- Green frosting
- Edible monster face decorations

Instructions:

1. Preheat your oven to 350°F (175°C) and line a cupcake pan with liners.
2. In a mixing bowl, combine the banana cake mix, eggs, vegetable oil, and mashed bananas. Mix until well combined.
3. Fill each cupcake liner 2/3 full with the batter.
4. Bake for 18-20 minutes or until a toothpick inserted comes out clean.
5. Let the cupcakes cool completely.

6. Frost each cupcake with green frosting.

7. Place edible monster face decorations on top for a monstrous look.

Summary: Monster Mash Banana Cupcakes are a playful and Halloween-themed treat. The monster face decorations add a fun and spooky element.

Tips and Tricks:

- Use different colored frosting for a variety of monster colors.

- Experiment with different expressions for the monster faces.

Candy Corn Creamsicle Cupcakes

Ingredients:

- 1 box of orange creamsicle cake mix
- 3 eggs
- 1/2 cup vegetable oil
- 1 cup buttermilk
- Orange frosting
- Yellow frosting
- White frosting
- Candy corn (for garnish)

Instructions:

1. Preheat your oven to 350°F (175°C) and line a cupcake pan with liners.
2. In a mixing bowl, combine the orange creamsicle cake mix, eggs, vegetable oil, and buttermilk. Mix until well combined.
3. Fill each cupcake liner 2/3 full with the batter.

4. Bake for 18-20 minutes or until a toothpick inserted comes out clean.

5. Let the cupcakes cool completely.

6. Frost some cupcakes with orange frosting, some with yellow frosting, and some with white frosting to mimic candy corn colors.

7. Garnish with a candy corn on top for a sweet touch.

Summary: Candy Corn Creamsicle Cupcakes are a colorful and Halloween-inspired treat. The candy corn colors and flavors make them reminiscent of the classic candy.

Tips and Tricks:

- Use a piping bag with a star tip to create a decorative swirl of frosting.
- Place the candy corn on top gently to avoid crushing it.

Vampire Bite Red Velvet Cupcakes

Ingredients:

- 1 box of red velvet cake mix
- 3 eggs
- 1/2 cup vegetable oil
- 1 cup buttermilk
- Red velvet frosting
- Edible vampire fang decorations
- Edible "blood" gel

Instructions:

1. Preheat your oven to 350°F (175°C) and line a cupcake pan with liners.
2. In a mixing bowl, combine the red velvet cake mix, eggs, vegetable oil, and buttermilk. Mix until smooth.
3. Fill each cupcake liner 2/3 full with the batter.
4. Bake for 18-20 minutes or until a toothpick inserted comes out clean.

5. Let the cupcakes cool completely.

6. Frost each cupcake with red velvet frosting.

7. Place edible vampire fang decorations on top for a vampire bite theme.

8. Add edible "blood" gel dripping from the fangs for a gory effect.

Summary: Vampire Bite Red Velvet Cupcakes are a spooky and delicious Halloween treat. The vampire fang decorations and "blood" gel add a chilling touch.

Tips and Tricks:

- Create a realistic "blood" effect by letting the gel drip down the sides of the cupcakes.
- Position the fang decorations carefully for a vampire bite appearance.

Pumpkin Patch Chocolate Cupcakes

Ingredients:

- 1 box of chocolate cake mix
- 3 eggs
- 1/2 cup vegetable oil
- 1 cup buttermilk
- Chocolate frosting
- Edible pumpkin patch decorations (mini pumpkins, edible dirt)

Instructions:

1. Preheat your oven to 350°F (175°C) and line a cupcake pan with liners.
2. In a mixing bowl, combine the chocolate cake mix, eggs, vegetable oil, and buttermilk. Mix until smooth.
3. Fill each cupcake liner 2/3 full with the batter.
4. Bake for 18-20 minutes or until a toothpick inserted comes out clean.

5. Let the cupcakes cool completely.

6. Frost each cupcake with chocolate frosting.

7. Decorate with edible pumpkin patch decorations, including mini pumpkins and edible "dirt."

Summary: Pumpkin Patch Chocolate Cupcakes are a delightful and festive Halloween treat. The pumpkin patch decorations make them resemble a real pumpkin patch.

Tips and Tricks:

- You can use crushed chocolate cookies for the edible "dirt" effect.

- Position the mini pumpkins creatively for a charming pumpkin patch scene.

Spiderweb Chocolate Orange Cupcakes

Ingredients:

- 1 box of chocolate orange cake mix
- 3 eggs
- 1/2 cup vegetable oil
- 1 cup buttermilk
- Chocolate orange frosting
- Black icing gel

Instructions:

1. Preheat your oven to 350°F (175°C) and line a cupcake pan with liners.
2. In a mixing bowl, combine the chocolate orange cake mix, eggs, vegetable oil, and buttermilk. Mix until well combined.
3. Fill each cupcake liner 2/3 full with the batter.
4. Bake for 18-20 minutes or until a toothpick inserted comes out clean.
5. Let the cupcakes cool completely.

6. Frost each cupcake with chocolate orange frosting.

7. Use black icing gel to create a spiderweb design on top of each cupcake.

Summary: Spiderweb Chocolate Orange Cupcakes are a flavorful and Halloween-themed treat. The chocolate orange flavor and spiderweb design add a spooky touch.

Tips and Tricks:

- Practice the spiderweb design on a piece of parchment paper before applying it to the cupcakes.

- You can add orange zest to the frosting for extra citrus flavor.

Caramel Apple Crisp Cupcakes

Ingredients:

- 1 box of apple crisp cake mix
- 3 eggs
- 1/2 cup vegetable oil
- 1 cup buttermilk
- Caramel frosting
- Mini apple crisp topping (crumbled)

Instructions:

1. Preheat your oven to 350°F (175°C) and line a cupcake pan with liners.
2. In a mixing bowl, combine the apple crisp cake mix, eggs, vegetable oil, and buttermilk. Mix until well combined.
3. Fill each cupcake liner 2/3 full with the batter.
4. Bake for 18-20 minutes or until a toothpick inserted comes out clean.
5. Let the cupcakes cool completely.

6. Frost each cupcake with caramel frosting.

7. Garnish with mini apple crisp topping for a crunchy and flavorful touch.

Summary: Caramel Apple Crisp Cupcakes are a delicious and autumn-inspired Halloween treat. The apple crisp topping and caramel frosting create a delightful combination.

Tips and Tricks:

- You can drizzle extra caramel sauce over the frosting for added caramel flavor.

- Serve these cupcakes with a scoop of vanilla ice cream for a true apple crisp experience.

Pumpkin Spice Latte Cupcakes

Ingredients:

- 1 box of pumpkin spice cake mix
- 3 eggs
- 1/2 cup vegetable oil
- 1 cup brewed coffee (cooled)
- Pumpkin spice frosting
- Cinnamon sticks (for garnish)

Instructions:

1. Preheat your oven to 350°F (175°C) and line a cupcake pan with liners.
2. In a mixing bowl, combine the pumpkin spice cake mix, eggs, vegetable oil, and brewed coffee. Mix until well combined.
3. Fill each cupcake liner 2/3 full with the batter.
4. Bake for 18-20 minutes or until a toothpick inserted comes out clean.
5. Let the cupcakes cool completely.

6. Frost each cupcake with pumpkin spice frosting.

7. Garnish with a small cinnamon stick on top for a latte-inspired touch.

Summary: Pumpkin Spice Latte Cupcakes are a delightful and cozy Halloween treat. The pumpkin spice and coffee flavors make them reminiscent of a latte.

Tips and Tricks:

- You can sprinkle a dash of ground cinnamon on top of the frosting for extra spice.

- Serve these cupcakes with a cup of coffee for the full latte experience.

Frankenstein's Monster Mint Cupcakes

Ingredients:

- 1 box of mint chocolate chip cake mix
- 3 eggs
- 1/2 cup vegetable oil
- 1 cup milk
- Mint chocolate frosting
- Edible Frankenstein face decorations

Instructions:

1. Preheat your oven to 350°F (175°C) and line a cupcake pan with liners.
2. In a mixing bowl, combine the mint chocolate chip cake mix, eggs, vegetable oil, and milk. Mix until well combined.
3. Fill each cupcake liner 2/3 full with the batter.
4. Bake for 18-20 minutes or until a toothpick inserted comes out clean.
5. Let the cupcakes cool completely.

6. Frost each cupcake with mint chocolate frosting.

7. Place edible Frankenstein face decorations on top for a monstrous Frankenstein look.

Summary: Frankenstein's Monster Mint Cupcakes are a spooky and minty Halloween treat. The Frankenstein face decorations add a fun and eerie touch.

Tips and Tricks:

- Use black icing gel to add extra details to the Frankenstein faces.

- Experiment with different expressions for the monsters.

Swamp Creature Green Tea Cupcakes

Ingredients:

- 1 box of green tea matcha cake mix
- 3 eggs
- 1/2 cup vegetable oil
- 1 cup milk
- Green tea frosting
- Edible swamp creature decorations

Instructions:

1. Preheat your oven to 350°F (175°C) and line a cupcake pan with liners.
2. In a mixing bowl, combine the green tea matcha cake mix, eggs, vegetable oil, and milk. Mix until well combined.
3. Fill each cupcake liner 2/3 full with the batter.
4. Bake for 18-20 minutes or until a toothpick inserted comes out clean.
5. Let the cupcakes cool completely.

6. Frost each cupcake with green tea frosting.

7. Place edible swamp creature decorations on top for a swampy and mysterious look.

Summary: Swamp Creature Green Tea Cupcakes are an exotic and Halloween-themed treat. The green tea flavor and swamp creature decorations create a mystical atmosphere.

Tips and Tricks:

- Experiment with different swamp creature decorations for variety.

- You can add a drop of green food coloring to the frosting for a brighter green color.

Candy Apple Cinnamon Cupcakes

Ingredients:

- 1 box of cinnamon apple cake mix
- 3 eggs
- 1/2 cup vegetable oil
- 1 cup buttermilk
- Cinnamon frosting
- Mini candy apple decorations

Instructions:

1. Preheat your oven to 350°F (175°C) and line a cupcake pan with liners.
2. In a mixing bowl, combine the cinnamon apple cake mix, eggs, vegetable oil, and buttermilk. Mix until well combined.
3. Fill each cupcake liner 2/3 full with the batter.
4. Bake for 18-20 minutes or until a toothpick inserted comes out clean.
5. Let the cupcakes cool completely.

6. Frost each cupcake with cinnamon frosting.

7. Place mini candy apple decorations on top for a sweet and festive look.

Summary: Candy Apple Cinnamon Cupcakes are a delicious and fall-inspired Halloween treat. The cinnamon flavor and candy apple decorations make them reminiscent of autumn.

Tips and Tricks:

- You can drizzle caramel sauce over the frosting for an extra candy apple touch.

- Position the mini candy apples creatively for a charming appearance.

Witches' Brew Green Punch

Ingredients:

- 2 cups lime sherbet
- 2 cups pineapple juice
- 2 cups lemon-lime soda
- Gummy worms (for garnish)
- Edible eyeball decorations

Instructions:

1. In a large punch bowl, add the lime sherbet.
2. Pour in the pineapple juice and lemon-lime soda.
3. Stir gently until well combined.
4. Garnish the punch with gummy worms and edible eyeball decorations.
5. Serve immediately and enjoy the "Witches' Brew"!

Summary: Witches' Brew Green Punch is a fun and spooky Halloween drink. The lime sherbet and gummy worms add a playful and eerie touch.

Tips and Tricks:

- You can add green food coloring for a more vibrant green color.
- Serve the punch in a cauldron for added effect.

Candy Corn Fruit Parfait

Ingredients:

- 1 cup pineapple chunks
- 1 cup mandarin orange segments
- 1 cup whipped cream or vanilla yogurt
- Candy corn (for garnish)

Instructions:

1. In a clear glass or parfait dish, layer pineapple chunks at the bottom.
2. Add a layer of mandarin orange segments on top of the pineapple.
3. Top with a layer of whipped cream or vanilla yogurt.
4. Repeat the layers until the glass is filled.
5. Garnish the top with candy corn for a festive touch.
6. Serve immediately and enjoy the Candy Corn Fruit Parfait!

Summary: Candy Corn Fruit Parfait is a colorful and healthy Halloween dessert. It captures the colors of candy corn in a delightful fruit parfait.

Tips and Tricks:

- You can use Greek yogurt for a protein-rich option.
- Add layers of other fruits like strawberries or grapes for variety.

Ghostly Banana Pops

Ingredients:

- Bananas
- White chocolate chips
- Mini chocolate chips (for eyes)
- Wooden popsicle sticks

Instructions:

1. Peel and cut the bananas in half.
2. Insert a wooden popsicle stick into the cut end of each banana half.
3. Place the bananas on a tray lined with parchment paper.
4. Melt the white chocolate chips in a microwave-safe bowl in 20-second intervals, stirring between each interval until smooth.
5. Dip each banana half into the melted white chocolate, covering it completely.
6. Quickly add two mini chocolate chips as eyes before the white chocolate sets.

7. Place the ghostly banana pops in the freezer to harden for about 2 hours.

8. Once frozen, they're ready to serve as spooky treats!

Summary: Ghostly Banana Pops are a simple and fun Halloween snack. They're perfect for kids and capture the essence of friendly ghosts.

Tips and Tricks:

- Use ripe bananas for a sweeter taste.
- You can drizzle dark chocolate over the frozen ghosts for added decoration.

Pumpkin Pie Dip with Apple Slices

Ingredients:

- 1 cup canned pumpkin puree
- 1 cup Greek yogurt
- 1/4 cup maple syrup
- 1 teaspoon pumpkin pie spice
- Apple slices (for dipping)

Instructions:

1. In a mixing bowl, combine the canned pumpkin puree, Greek yogurt, maple syrup, and pumpkin pie spice. Mix until smooth.
2. Chill the dip in the refrigerator for at least 30 minutes before serving.
3. Serve the pumpkin pie dip with apple slices for a tasty and healthy Halloween snack.

Summary: Pumpkin Pie Dip with Apple Slices is a creamy and flavorful Halloween treat. It's a lighter alternative to traditional pumpkin pie.

Tips and Tricks:

- You can also serve the dip with graham crackers or cinnamon pita chips.

- Adjust the sweetness by adding more or less maple syrup to taste.

Ghostly Meringue Cookies

Ingredients:

- 3 large egg whites
- 3/4 cup granulated sugar
- 1/2 teaspoon vanilla extract
- Mini chocolate chips (for eyes)

Instructions:

1. Preheat your oven to 200°F (93°C) and line a baking sheet with parchment paper.
2. In a clean, dry mixing bowl, beat the egg whites until they form stiff peaks.
3. Gradually add the granulated sugar while continuing to beat the egg whites until the mixture is glossy and holds its shape.
4. Add the vanilla extract and gently fold it into the mixture.
5. Spoon or pipe the meringue mixture onto the prepared baking sheet to create ghost shapes.
6. Place mini chocolate chips as eyes on each ghost.

7. Bake in the preheated oven for 1.5 to 2 hours, or until the meringue cookies are crisp and dry.

8. Let them cool completely before removing them from the parchment paper.

Summary: Ghostly Meringue Cookies are a delightful and spooky Halloween treat. These light and airy cookies are perfect for parties and gatherings.

Tips and Tricks:

- Ensure there are no traces of egg yolk in the egg whites for the best results.

- You can add a drop of black food coloring to the meringue mixture for a grayish ghostly appearance.

Caramel Apple Dip

Ingredients:

- 1/2 cup creamy peanut butter
- 1/2 cup caramel sauce
- 1/4 cup chopped peanuts
- Sliced apples (for dipping)

Instructions:

1. In a microwave-safe bowl, heat the peanut butter for about 30 seconds or until it's easy to stir.
2. Stir in the caramel sauce until well combined.
3. Sprinkle chopped peanuts on top.
4. Serve the caramel apple dip with sliced apples for a delicious and indulgent Halloween snack.

Summary: Caramel Apple Dip is a sweet and nutty Halloween treat that pairs perfectly with fresh apple slices.

Tips and Tricks:

- Drizzle extra caramel sauce on top for added sweetness.

- You can use almond butter or any nut butter of your choice.

Pumpkin Spice Popcorn

Ingredients:

- 10 cups popped popcorn (about 1/2 cup unpopped kernels)
- 1/4 cup unsalted butter
- 1/4 cup brown sugar
- 1 teaspoon pumpkin pie spice
- 1/2 teaspoon vanilla extract

Instructions:

1. Preheat your oven to 250°F (120°C) and line a large baking sheet with parchment paper.
2. In a saucepan, melt the butter over low heat.
3. Stir in the brown sugar, pumpkin pie spice, and vanilla extract until the mixture is smooth.
4. Pour the caramel sauce over the popped popcorn and gently toss to coat.
5. Spread the coated popcorn on the prepared baking sheet.

6. Bake in the preheated oven for 45 minutes, stirring every 15 minutes.

7. Let the pumpkin spice popcorn cool completely before serving.

Summary: Pumpkin Spice Popcorn is a crunchy and flavorful Halloween snack. It's perfect for movie nights and gatherings.

Tips and Tricks:

- You can add a sprinkle of sea salt for a sweet and salty combination.

- Customize the recipe by adding your favorite nuts or candies.

Spiderweb Guacamole

Ingredients:

- 2 ripe avocados
- 1 small red onion, finely diced
- 1-2 cloves garlic, minced
- 1 small tomato, diced
- 1 lime, juiced
- Salt and pepper to taste
- Black olives (for spiderweb decoration)

Instructions:

1. Cut the avocados in half, remove the pits, and scoop the flesh into a bowl.
2. Mash the avocado with a fork until it reaches your desired consistency.
3. Stir in the diced red onion, minced garlic, diced tomato, and lime juice.
4. Season with salt and pepper to taste.

5. Transfer the guacamole to a serving plate and smooth it out.

6. Use sliced black olives to create a spiderweb design on top of the guacamole.

7. Serve with tortilla chips or vegetable sticks.

Summary: Spiderweb Guacamole is a festive and spooky Halloween dip. It's a creative way to enjoy a classic favorite with a Halloween twist.

Tips and Tricks:

- Use a toothpick or skewer to help create the spiderweb design with precision.

- You can add diced jalapeños for a spicy kick.

Mummy Hot Dogs

Ingredients:

- Hot dogs
- Crescent roll dough
- Mustard or ketchup (for eyes)

Instructions:

1. Preheat your oven according to the crescent roll dough package instructions.
2. Unroll the crescent roll dough and separate it into triangles.
3. Wrap each hot dog with a triangle of crescent roll dough, leaving a small gap near one end for the "face."
4. Place the wrapped hot dogs on a baking sheet.
5. Bake in the preheated oven as per the crescent roll dough package instructions, or until the dough is golden brown.
6. Once baked, use mustard or ketchup to create eyes on the mummy hot dogs.

7. Serve them as a fun and savory Halloween snack.

Summary: Mummy Hot Dogs are a playful and savory Halloween treat. They're great for kids and adults alike.

Tips and Tricks:

- Experiment with different condiments for the eyes, like mayonnaise or ranch dressing.

- You can add cheese inside the hot dogs for extra flavor.

Haunted Halloween Punch

Ingredients:

- 2 cups grape juice
- 2 cups orange soda
- 2 cups lemon-lime soda
- Raspberry sherbet
- Gummy worms (for garnish)
- Edible eyeball decorations

Instructions:

1. In a large punch bowl, combine the grape juice, orange soda, and lemon-lime soda.
2. Add scoops of raspberry sherbet to the punch mixture.
3. Garnish the punch with gummy worms and edible eyeball decorations.
4. Serve the Haunted Halloween Punch in glasses with ice.

Summary: Haunted Halloween Punch is a colorful and spooky drink that's perfect for Halloween parties and gatherings.

Tips and Tricks:

- Use dry ice for a misty and eerie effect (handle with care and do not consume).
- You can substitute raspberry sherbet with any other fruit sorbet.

Witch Hat Cookies

Ingredients:

- Chocolate wafer cookies
- Hershey's Kisses
- Orange frosting (or icing)
- Sprinkles (for decoration)

Instructions:

1. Unwrap the Hershey's Kisses.
2. Using a small amount of orange frosting, attach the flat side of a Hershey's Kiss to the center of a chocolate wafer cookie to create a witch hat.
3. Apply a small amount of orange frosting around the base of the Hershey's Kiss to secure it in place.
4. Use additional orange frosting to create a decorative band around the base of the Hershey's Kiss, just like a witch hat.
5. Add sprinkles for extra decoration, if desired.
6. Let the witch hat cookies set until the frosting hardens.

Summary: Witch Hat Cookies are a simple and cute Halloween dessert. They're a delightful addition to any Halloween-themed event.

Tips and Tricks:

- Experiment with different colored frosting for a variety of witch hat styles.
- You can use mini peanut butter cups instead of Hershey's Kisses for a nutty twist.

Pumpkin Rice Krispie Treats

Ingredients:

- 3 tablespoons unsalted butter
- 4 cups mini marshmallows
- 6 cups Rice Krispies cereal
- Orange food coloring
- Pretzel sticks
- Green M&M's or chocolate chips (for stems)

Instructions:

1. In a large saucepan, melt the butter over low heat.
2. Add the mini marshmallows and stir until they are completely melted and the mixture is smooth.
3. Tint the marshmallow mixture with orange food coloring to achieve the desired pumpkin color.
4. Remove the saucepan from heat and stir in the Rice Krispies cereal until well coated.
5. Using greased hands or a greased cookie cutter, shape the mixture into pumpkin-shaped treats.

6. Insert a pretzel stick into the top of each treat as a stem.

7. Place a green M&M or chocolate chip at the base of the pretzel stick as a leaf.

8. Let the pumpkin Rice Krispie treats cool and set before serving.

Summary: Pumpkin Rice Krispie Treats are a playful and crispy Halloween snack. They're perfect for kids and adults who love classic Rice Krispie treats with a seasonal twist.

Tips and Tricks:

- Use a silicone pumpkin mold for uniform pumpkin shapes.
- You can add cinnamon or pumpkin pie spice to the mixture for extra flavor.

Creepy Crawly Deviled Eggs

Ingredients:

- 6 hard-boiled eggs, peeled and halved
- 2 tablespoons mayonnaise
- 1 teaspoon Dijon mustard
- Salt and pepper to taste
- Black olives (for spiders)

Instructions:

1. Cut a small slice from the bottom of each egg half to make them sit flat.
2. Carefully remove the yolks and place them in a bowl.
3. Mash the yolks with mayonnaise, Dijon mustard, salt, and pepper until smooth.
4. Spoon or pipe the yolk mixture back into the egg whites.
5. Slice black olives to create spider bodies and legs, then place them on top of the deviled eggs.

6. Serve the Creepy Crawly Deviled Eggs as a spooky and savory Halloween appetizer.

Summary: Creepy Crawly Deviled Eggs are a ghoulish twist on a classic appetizer. They're a fun addition to Halloween parties and gatherings.

Tips and Tricks:

- Use a pastry bag with a star tip to pipe the yolk mixture for an elegant presentation.

- You can add a dash of paprika for extra flavor and color.

Candy Corn Jello Cups

Ingredients:

- Orange Jello
- Lemon Jello
- Whipped cream (optional)
- Candy corn (for garnish)

Instructions:

1. Prepare the orange Jello according to the package instructions and pour it into serving cups.

2. Let the orange Jello set in the refrigerator for about 2 hours or until it's partially set.

3. Prepare the lemon Jello according to the package instructions and gently pour it over the partially set orange Jello.

4. Return the cups to the refrigerator and let them set completely.

5. Serve the Candy Corn Jello Cups with a dollop of whipped cream and garnish with candy corn for a festive Halloween dessert.

Summary: Candy Corn Jello Cups are a colorful and whimsical Halloween dessert. They capture the iconic candy corn colors in a fun and wobbly treat.

Tips and Tricks:

- You can use sugar-free Jello for a lower-calorie option.
- Experiment with different flavors and colors for variety.

Thank you

Printed in Great Britain
by Amazon